The Boundary Blueprint

Praise for *The Boundary Blueprint*

This book is a boundary-setting bible for women who want to lead with clarity, courage and compassion. It's equal parts insightful, practical and deeply personal. With honesty and heart, Julia gives nuance to what so many women struggle to navigate — with permission and power — and offers a way forward that's practical, achievable and long overdue. A must-read for women in STEM, leadership and life.

— **Anneli Blundell, Author of *The Gender Penalty***

The Boundary Blueprint inspires us to improve our lives by setting clear boundaries. Julia supports the reader with practical strategies in every chapter. Like a friend, she talks through different circumstances, leading the way with anecdotes, and providing understanding and guidance. The questions at the end of the chapter really helped me reflect and see things through a new lens. This is definitely a book to read with pen and paper — I made many notes and reflections! Thank you, Julia, for sharing these tools and tips. I feel better equipped with tools to face my challenges of parenting and guiding STEM graduates at work while balancing postgraduate studies.

— **Fiona Carter, Aerospace Engineer, Early Career Specialist at Nova Systems**

As Julia clearly outlines, boundaries are linked to resilience and grit in a very important way. I particularly liked the individual stories, especially Julia's personal stories, which are the best possible examples to learn from. Any person in an underrepresented field can learn from this book.

— **Pamela Melroy, Astronaut and Former NASA Deputy Administrator**

I love the quotes at the start of each chapter and the questions at the end—they really help the message sink in and make me think about how it applies to my own life.

— **Suzanna Olofsson, Aerospace Engineer**

I found *The Boundary Blueprint* a valuable starting point for thinking through the challenges women often face in STEM and male-dominated industries. The neurodivergent lens was especially insightful, and the discussion on boundaries raised important questions about how we bring these ideas into real workplace conversations.

— **Gail Fulton, Director, CSIRO Science Connect**

The Boundary Blueprint

Transforming Your Life, One Limit at a Time

JULIA GIBNEY

Published by Julia Gibney

First published in 2025 in Melbourne, Australia

Copyright © 2025 Julia Gibney

The moral rights of the author have been asserted.

All rights reserved. No part of this book may be used or reproduced by any means (graphic, electronic or mechanical, including photocopying or recording) or by any information storage and/or retrieval system without the prior written permission of the copyright owner.

For author queries or further information, visit www.winterandassociates.com.au

Edited by Jenny Magee

Typeset and printed in Australia by BookPOD

ISBN: 978-0-6459980-2-3 (paperback) ISBN: 978-0-6459980-3-0 (e-book)

 A catalogue record for this book is available from the National Library of Australia

This book was written for a special woman.

You know who you are.

Just remember, transforming your life, one limit at a time, is like a butterfly emerging from its cocoon. Each struggle against the walls of the cocoon represents overcoming fear and setting boundaries, building the strength needed to fly. Every challenge faced is another strand torn away, revealing your true potential. Though the journey is slow and sometimes painful, each small breakthrough brings you closer to the freedom of spreading your wings and learning to fly.

CONTENTS

Important notice	xiii
Preface	xv
Introduction	1
The Crucial Role of Boundaries for Women	1
How to use this book	6
CHAPTER 1: Understanding Yourself	**7**
Self-awareness versus awareness of self	9
You don't have to do it alone	13
CHAPTER 2: The Ripple Effect of Boundaries	**17**
Understanding your boundaries	18
Connecting your boundaries to your values	19
The influence of role models on boundaries	20
How boundaries change over time	21
Boundary violations are a human issue	21
You are not your parents	22
Recognising how boundaries help or hurt	24
Overcoming guilt	24
The hidden effects of boundary crossing on those we love	26
Understanding the ripple effect	29
CHAPTER 3: Resilience and Grit	**31**
Evolving grit and resilience	33
Cultivating resilience for sustained success	35

CHAPTER 4 — 39
Navigating Societal Expectations — 39
Equality, equity and social justice — 40
Knowing what society expects — 43
Navigating external influences — 44
Recognising workplace dynamics — 53
Myths around women's assertiveness — 58
The impact of external pressures on wellbeing and self-worth — 60

CHAPTER 5: Boundary Foundations — 65
Elements of a boundary — 66
Distinct types of boundaries — 69
Relational boundaries — 81

CHAPTER 6: Trigger Points — 91
Understanding your response to boundary violations — 93
Navigating neurodiversity — 94
Trauma responses to boundary violations — 96
Why do we respond the way we do? — 105
Suggested responses to boundary violations — 109

CHAPTER 7: Setting Strong Boundaries — 115
Recognising your patterns — 115
Boundary diagnostic — 128

CHAPTER 8: Challenging Gender Bias — 133
Historical gender barriers — 134
Missing mentors — 135
The double-bind — 136
Common stereotypes of women in STEM — 138
Fostering an inclusive work environment — 146

Breaking the cycle	148
Building an inclusive culture	156

CHAPTER 9: Professional Boundaries — 167

Government support for gender equality	168
Nurturing the garden	168
Defining professional boundaries	169
Personal boundaries in professional settings	170
Employee turnover affects organisational stability	176
The positive impact of employee departures	179
Handling workplace dynamics	180
Getting the right balance	191
The negative impacts of overstepping boundaries	192
Other strategies when work boundaries are crossed	201

CHAPTER 10: The Balancing Act — 209

Identifying signs of burnout	211
Your values are the key to balance	214
Work-life balance in STEM	217

CHAPTER 11: Digital Boundaries — 243

The positive impact of digital technology	245
The negative impact on mental health	248
Impacts on personal and professional relationships	249
Creating healthy digital habits	250
Pushing back online and in-person	253

CHAPTER 12: Intentional Networking — 255

Building a strong professional network	256
Don't step on their toes	261
The balancing act	262
Balancing networking with family commitments	267

And Finally …	273
Three steps to success	274
Rebuilding after a setback	275
Renew, review, change, repeat	276
Let me help you	276
Appendix 1: Values Identification Exercise	279
Appendix 2: Parenting Programs and Resource Guide	282
Appendix 3: Domestic and Family Violence Support Services	284
Appendix 4: Recommended Readings	287
Appendix 5: Extra Resources to Learn Assertiveness Skills	290
Appendix 6: Self-Evaluation of Your Work-Life Balance	294
Appendix 7: Wheel of Life	299
References	301

Important notice

This book is designed to assist the reader with strategies to establish and maintain effective boundaries. Some parts of this book encourage self-reflection and growth, sometimes with the help of a coach. Therefore, I want to clarify the difference between coaching and counselling.

Coaching emphasises a forward-looking approach to facilitating development and growth through short-, medium- and long-term objectives and achievable goals. Working with a coach or mentor who employs illuminating and perceptive questioning methods can assist in devising strategies for success. Coaching and mentoring can support progress towards clearly defined objectives.

In contrast, therapy and counselling delve into the past and address aspects of an individual's life that could benefit from the expertise of qualified mental health professionals who assess your specific needs and provide tailored guidance.

While I wish you every success, I make no guarantees about the results of the ideas and resources presented within these pages. It is meant to be informative and thought-provoking and intended to complement, not replace, the expertise of counsellors, therapists and psychologists. Seeking professional advice is an essential step in making informed choices that are best suited to individual circumstances. Your ultimate success or failure will be the result of your efforts, your particular situation and circumstances.

Preface

Writing this book on boundaries has been an incredible journey; it has challenged me in ways I never anticipated. Boundaries are deeply personal, so researching and reflecting on this topic stirred emotions and memories I hadn't fully processed. During the writing process, I grappled with certain topics and sought the help of a psychologist to navigate the emotions that surfaced.

It was during this time that I received a diagnosis of autism and ADHD (Attention Deficit Hyperactivity Disorder). That insight has profoundly shaped my understanding of myself and the world around me. A common aspect of both autism and ADHD is hypersensitivity, which can manifest in various ways. For me, one particularly notable symptom that has often caught me by surprise has been Rejection-Sensitive Dysphoria (RSD), where even small perceived rejections or criticisms feel overwhelming. Additionally, I have had moments of seemingly non-obvious (to others) meltdowns or outbursts when the sensory overload or stress becomes too much to handle. This discovery has significantly influenced how I framed my personal perspectives shared throughout this book. It also gave me a unique lens to explore boundaries, especially how they pertain to neurodivergent individuals like myself.

While this book reflects my experiences and insights, I want to acknowledge that others who are neurodivergent may have very different experiences. My thirty-year career in the fields of Science, Technology, Engineering and Mathematics (STEM), coupled with my recent diagnosis, has led me to suspect that the prevalence of neurodivergence within the field of STEM is significantly higher than the national estimated average of 20%.[1,2,3,4] Some studies suggest that traits associated with neurodivergence, such as strong analytical and systematic thinking, may predispose individuals towards careers in technical fields like computer science, engineering and mathematics.[5]

However, many neurodivergent individuals remain unaware of their neurodivergence, with some estimates suggesting that up to 50% of those affected are undiagnosed or unaware of their condition.[6] Based on my experiences and interactions with others, I would place it closer to 40-50%, with a majority undiagnosed. I am now exploring this hypothesis through my postgraduate doctorate research. It is a crucial area of study because, while some perceive neurodivergence as a disability, I have encountered highly distinguished and exceptionally intellectual individuals who view it not as a limitation but as a different way of processing and interpreting the world. This unique cognitive approach shapes how we engage with problems, innovate and contribute to STEM fields.

My goal in calling this out is not to generalise. Rather, I want to provide readers with an additional layer of understanding. Throughout the book, you'll find references to how neurodivergent individuals may perceive situations differently or approach boundary-setting in ways that might contrast with neurotypical perspectives. I have included a list of recommended readings on communication styles and supportive environments for neurodivergent individuals in Appendix 4.

Preface

By sharing these perspectives, I hope to foster greater empathy and understanding of the diverse ways we navigate boundaries in our lives. Thank you for joining me on this journey. I hope this book provides the insights and tools you need to embrace boundaries that support your wellbeing.

Julia

Introduction

The Crucial Role of Boundaries for Women

When we fail to set boundaries and hold people accountable, we feel used and mistreated.
— Brené Brown [7]

Children begin learning about boundaries as early as toddlerhood; at around eighteen months to two years, they start asserting preferences and developing autonomy. By the time they start school they can understand complex boundaries, such as emotional or social limits, but may not always feel empowered to enforce them. That often depends on how they are raised and socialised, as strict or dismissive environments can hinder their ability to advocate for themselves. Supporting children in setting boundaries through modelling respectful behaviour, validating their feelings and teaching them how to express themselves is essential for fostering their self-worth and confidence.

Similarly, women's boundaries are shaped by societal expectations, gender norms and caregiving roles, which create unique challenges in asserting personal limits. In a world where work and home life often overlap, women must navigate competing demands while maintaining boundaries, particularly in male-dominated workplaces. From navigating professional expectations to fulfilling family responsibilities, clear boundaries are vital.

I am often asked what gives me strength. How do I handle challenging situations, and what advice would I give younger people to help them be assertive without being aggressive or anxious?

The advice I would have given my twenty-five-year-old self is quite different from what I share today. I used to struggle to stand up for myself, but in recent years, I have learned the importance of valuing myself and staying true to my beliefs. Once I mastered standing for myself, it became easier when somebody challenged my rights, opinions or boundaries. This growth inspired me to write this book and share these insights.

Standing *for* yourself and standing *up* for yourself are distinct yet equally vital aspects of self-empowerment. The former is about internal alignment — staying true to your values and making choices that honour your identity and goals. The latter involves external advocacy — asserting your needs and boundaries, especially when challenged. Understanding and practising both are essential for maintaining authenticity and resilience in the face of life's demands. This book explores why these concepts matter and how they shape your personal and professional journey. It also discusses the balance women must strike between their career ambitions and personal obligations. Through anecdotes, insights and practical strategies, I will clarify how boundaries empower women to thrive in the workplace and at home.

Introduction: The Crucial Role of Boundaries for Women

While many people struggle with setting boundaries, I focus on the pressures and biases women incur in male-dominated workplaces and how these affect their personal lives. Some topics may apply to everyone, but others are unique to women. This book reflects my perspective, and I understand that others may have different views. Join me on a journey of self-discovery and empowerment as we explore the importance of boundaries for women in today's complex world.

But before we discuss the importance of boundaries, we need to ask what they are and why they should matter.

In simple terms, boundaries define where we end and others begin; they are invisible lines that shape how we interact with the world.

> **Boundaries define where we end and others begin.**

They provide structure, protect our wellbeing and communicate what behaviours we will or will not accept. Boundaries are essential for self-care, helping us protect our time, energy and emotions. They allow us to set limits, assert our needs and maintain healthy relationships.

Boundaries are crucial to self-respect, helping us prioritise our wellbeing and confidently pursue our goals. If your boundaries are too firm, you may face resistance from others who want to help, or you might stay stuck in your ways, unable to grow. Yet without clear boundaries, you risk feeling overwhelmed and drained and unable to prioritise your needs. It can lead to burnout, being taken advantage of, and resentment in your work and personal lives.

Blurred boundaries can cause misunderstandings and conflicts, harming relationships.

Societal expectations, fear of conflict, people-pleasing tendencies and cultural conditioning can make it hard to assert your boundaries, thus sacrificing your happiness. A lack of confidence and self-worth can also stop you from backing yourself. Without clear boundaries, personal growth, self-esteem and opportunities for success and happiness may be limited.

Setting boundaries is like building a fence around your garden. Without a fence, your garden is exposed and can easily be trampled — having no boundaries leaves you vulnerable. A strong brick wall protects your flowers but hides their beauty from others. Firm boundaries protect you but may keep others at a distance. A picket fence allows others to admire your efforts while offering protection. Such flexible boundaries protect your values

Introduction: The Crucial Role of Boundaries for Women

and desires while maintaining self-respect and personal growth, creating space for genuine and meaningful connections.

A PERSONAL PERSPECTIVE

When I was eight years old, an event made me realise how scared I was to speak up and enforce a boundary, even when I felt something wasn't fair. My bedroom was my favourite place to play and be myself. But my dad didn't like how messy it was at times. He had really strict rules, and I was too afraid to question them.

One day, he told me to clean my room or there would be consequences. I was scared. I didn't know exactly what he meant, but I didn't want to find out. I just wanted it to look neat enough to keep him happy, so I thought I was clever when I shoved my toys under the bed and in the wardrobe. Then I went out on my bike with my sister, hoping it would all blow over.

When we got back, everything felt wrong. My room was empty. My favourite toys, my books — everything was gone. I ran to the backyard and saw the worst thing I could imagine. There were my things, burning in a big pile. I wanted to cry, scream or beg him to stop, but I couldn't. I just stood there, frozen, terrified that speaking up would only make it worse.

That day hurt more than I can say. It wasn't just about losing my things. It felt like my room, my safe space, wasn't mine anymore. I learned to keep quiet and to hide how I felt because I believed standing up for myself wasn't worth the risk. It took me a long time to understand how much that moment shaped how I saw myself and how I trusted people.

This personal perspective provides context on how others' actions shape our self-perception, behaviour and attitude towards setting and maintaining boundaries as we grow. It is not meant to seek sympathy but to show why I behaved a certain way before understanding the importance of setting boundaries. Everyone's experiences are unique and individuality should be valued.

How to use this book

I've designed this book as a guide to understanding and enforcing boundaries, offering practical strategies to set and maintain them in both personal and professional settings. It starts with foundational concepts and then builds on actionable strategies to create healthier relationships. As you read on, specific sections — such as navigating neurodiversity, personal perspectives and case studies — provide examples and context. You can read the book sequentially or focus on chapters that meet your immediate needs. All offer valuable insights to support your boundary-setting journey.

Understanding Yourself

The better you know yourself, the better your relationship with the rest of the world.
— Toni Collette [8]

My dad thought he was teaching me a valuable life lesson. He had no idea of the lasting impact his actions would have on me. When we interact with others, our intentions may be good, but the impact of our words and actions can be very different, leaving unintended emotional scars on others, especially those we love most.

Self-awareness safeguards our emotional wellbeing and fosters healthier, more balanced relationships by minimising unintentional harm and creating opportunities for mutual respect and growth. When considering boundaries, we must think carefully before compromising them for someone we don't respect or know well.

It has taken decades for my dad and me to understand what went wrong and to heal the rift between us.

Relationships are nuanced, and a win/lose scenario may cost more in the long run. While standing firm might be worthwhile if there's much to gain, aiming for a win/win outcome where both sides benefit is the ideal solution. If things don't go as planned or you act too quickly (as I've done before), take some time to reflect on the lessons learned. Observe how others behave and react and consider if they consistently align with their actions — insight is valuable for managing relationships with unpredictable or insincere individuals.

Consider the dynamics of your relationships. How well do you know yourself and others? Are your perceptions clear or clouded by preconceived ideas? I faced many challenges when I was younger because I lacked self-awareness and role models. That was before I understood that I saw the world differently because I was neurodivergent. Sometimes, I overreacted or said things that were taken out of context. Without strong networks to guide me, I had to learn through trial and error. Recently we've learned that my dad had similar challenges. If only we'd both known then what we know now.

Today, I have supportive communities that allow me to operate authentically. I have valuable insights and tools that have allowed me to manage interactions with clarity and purpose. That is why I have written this book: to show you that you, too, can carve your own path, be strong, assert your boundaries and stay true to yourself. But doing it alone takes much longer — it took me twenty-five extra years. Why spend that precious time when you can learn from others' experiences and gain valuable lessons without facing the same hardships?

> Your uniqueness makes you who you are!

My goal is not to tell you the 'right' way to do things but to stress the importance of finding what works best for you. After all, your uniqueness makes you who you are!

Self-awareness versus awareness of self

Self-awareness is the ability to recognise and understand your thoughts, emotions, behaviours and tendencies. It involves reflecting on your thoughts and behaviours to gain insight into your motivations, strengths, weaknesses and values. This self-understanding promotes personal growth, better decision-making and stronger relationships.

Awareness of self is different. It refers to how you see yourself in relation to the outside world, including other people, situations and societal norms. It includes understanding your internal thoughts and emotions, and external influences like culture, social dynamics and environmental factors.

Tasha Eurich, a well-known organisational psychologist and author, explores self-awareness in her book *Insight*.[9] Her research identifies seven aspects of self-awareness, including knowing your values, passions and aspirations, your role in your environment, your reactions to others and your impact on those around you. Understanding these characteristics helps reveal hidden barriers that block our self-understanding and awareness of others.

Dr Eurich's surveys show a major gap between perceived and actual self-awareness. While 95% of people think they are self-aware, her research found that less than 15% truly are. This finding highlights the need to distinguish between self-awareness and awareness of self, as many overestimate their understanding of their behaviours and their impact on others. Eurich points out that societal influences create blind spots, making it harder for people to recognise their own and others' boundaries. People may struggle to set or respect boundaries, harming communication and relationships without genuine self-awareness.

Intent versus impact

To fully understand how you show up to others, it's essential to consider both your intent and your impact. While self-awareness provides insight into your internal world, awareness of self in relation to others helps you recognise how your actions (intentional or not) are perceived and affect those around you. Both are needed to foster meaningful connections and ensure your interactions align with your values and objectives.

Intent is the reason or motivation behind someone's actions, whether at work or in personal life. For example, you might intend to give feedback at work to help a colleague improve. In personal situations, you might intend to support a friend during tough times.

Chapter 1: Understanding Yourself

However, the impact of actions can vary depending on your level of self-awareness. If you have low self-awareness, you may not fully understand how your behaviour affects others. In contrast, if you are more self-aware, you are more likely to recognise the potential consequences of your actions and adjust your behaviour to ensure your intentions match the desired impact.

Therefore, impact refers to the actual effect that our actions have on others, whether at work or in personal relationships. It includes how actions are perceived and experienced. For example, even with good intentions, giving unsolicited advice at work might cause discomfort or resentment. Similarly, in personal relationships, offering advice without being asked may suggest a lack of trust in the other person's ability to handle their challenges, affecting the relationship dynamic.

That's crossing boundaries.

When we lack self-awareness or our intent does not align with our impact, the effect can be more significant than we realise. For example, we may think we are offering support or advice, but the person receiving it might feel misunderstood, unsupported or even patronised. This disconnect between intent and impact can lead to unintended emotional harm, creating tension and resentment.

Those closest to us, such as family members or close friends, are often most affected because they are more vulnerable to our actions. Failure to recognise how our words, actions or behaviours are perceived can erode trust, damage emotional safety and even strain long-term connections.

PERSONAL REFLECTION

When reflecting on my parenting style and its impact on my daughters as they were growing up, I've come to recognise that my behaviour and words — though intended to be supportive or humorous — often had an entirely different effect than I anticipated, sometimes causing unintended harm.

One incident, almost a decade ago, still stands out. During a shopping trip, my daughter asked for KFC for lunch, and I jokingly said she might turn into a chicken if she kept eating it. Her immediate reaction of tears and a visible change in body language showed the impact of my words. Despite my apology, this moment led her to avoid KFC for a long time and overly focus on diet and exercise, highlighting the lasting effects of my comment.

Chapter 1: Understanding Yourself

> *This experience prompted me to reflect deeply on my intent and its impact on my daughter. I failed to see that she would not perceive my remarks as the joke I intended.*

Even when our actions or comments are well intended or said in jest, the impact can still be perceived as a boundary violation if they disregard the other person's needs, feelings or personal space. Without recognising how our behaviour and words affect others, we may inadvertently cross a line that undermines trust and emotional safety, demonstrating how intent and impact do not always align.

You don't have to do it alone

As you learn to set and maintain appropriate boundaries, it's important to remember that you don't have to navigate this process alone. Ask for help; you gain a lot by learning from others. Seek out mentors and colleagues for guidance. I have gained valuable insights from people who, though not perfect, taught me about self-awareness and perspective. Staying true to yourself is essential when standing up for yourself, and your authenticity can inspire others around you.

I had very few role models in STEM early in my career. Now, as a woman aged over fifty, my journey has taught me valuable lessons about resilience, grit and assertiveness. I want to share these lessons to help young women in male-dominated industries stand up for themselves and maintain their boundaries. I also want to encourage men to support their female colleagues and treat them as equals. It is not about us versus them; but about working together to create a more inclusive, supportive environment for everyone.

Women in male-dominated industries face challenges asserting their needs and protecting their wellbeing. However, having strategies to uphold boundaries is vital to creating a respectful and empowering workplace. That protects your mental and emotional health and shows others how you expect to be treated.

Current estimates by the World Economic Forum suggest that achieving workplace equality will take more than 135 years.[10] When I joined the military in 1994, I would have guessed it was around 150 years, so very little has changed in the last thirty years. To speed up progress, we must support each other, be true to ourselves and assert our boundaries without guilt to reduce the gender gap and create a better future for everyone.

To conclude this chapter, take a moment to reflect on how you present yourself to others. The following guiding questions are designed to help you explore the impact of your communication and actions. While this reflection may feel uncomfortable, it is essential for deepening your self-awareness and understanding how your words and behaviours influence those around you. By examining both conscious and unconscious boundary crossings, you can gain insights into the effects of your interactions and better understand the importance of maintaining healthy boundaries in your personal and professional life.

Chapter 1: Understanding Yourself

 Guiding questions

1. How do I respect others' personal space and physical boundaries? When might I have unintentionally invaded their space?

2. How am I mindful of others' emotional boundaries and sensitive topics? Where might I have overstepped by prying into personal matters or offering unsolicited advice?

3. How attentive am I to verbal and nonverbal cues indicating discomfort or resistance from others, and how might I have disregarded these signs in the past?

4. How do I consider the impact of my words and actions on others' wellbeing and autonomy?

5. How open am I to feedback? Am I willing to adjust my behaviour based on others' boundaries and preferences? How do I respond when confronted about boundary violations?

The Ripple Effect of Boundaries

People need to learn that their actions do affect other people. So, be careful what you say and do. It's not always just about you.

— Author unknown

Have you thrown a stone into a pond and watched the ripples? Our words and actions are like that. They have far wider effects than we realise, influencing those we raise and those we work with or meet socially. While managing our own boundaries, we must also respect others' boundaries with care and empathy. Even small actions, like my untimely KFC quip to my daughter, can leave lasting impressions.

This chapter is designed to help you reflect on your boundaries — their origins, how they align with your values and how others have shaped them. We'll also consider how boundaries evolve over time.

Understanding your boundaries

Understanding your boundaries starts with reflecting on your values, needs and non-negotiables. These define what feels safe, respectful and acceptable in your personal and professional interactions. They help you protect your time, energy and emotional wellbeing while maintaining healthy relationships.

As you consider what boundaries matter most to you, think about situations where you've felt uncomfortable, drained or disrespected — these moments often reveal areas where boundaries are needed. Chapter Five will cover the different types of boundaries, providing insight as to where you may have not considered some types of behaviours actually violate your or others' boundaries. For now, start thinking about what you're unwilling to compromise when it comes to your wellbeing and interactions with others.

Connecting your boundaries to your values

Your boundaries directly reflect your core values. They help you define what's acceptable and align your actions with your principles. For example, if you value honesty, you may set boundaries around how you expect to be communicated with or how you handle sensitive topics. Similarly, if balance is a priority, you might establish boundaries around work hours to protect your personal time. Identifying your values provides clarity and empowers you to uphold boundaries that reinforce your identity and wellbeing. Understanding this connection makes it easier to stay firm when others challenge your boundaries.

> Your boundaries directly reflect your core values.

If you haven't yet explored your values, I encourage you to complete the values identification exercise in Appendix 1. This will clarify what matters most to you and help you better understand the foundation of your boundaries.

The influence of role models on boundaries

Who were your role models growing up? What did they do — or not do — that left lasting memories?

Whether positive or negative, those people will have significantly influenced how you set and enact your boundaries. Positive role models who respect their limits and teach others to do the same are powerful examples of how healthy boundaries contribute to wellbeing. Aside from family members, these role models might include past teachers, mentors or colleagues who exemplify assertiveness and self-respect. They teach by action, showing that setting boundaries is not only possible but necessary for maintaining balance and fulfilling relationships.

In contrast, negative role models can hinder your ability to set boundaries effectively. If you grew up with people who neglected their own needs or were very domineering, who overextended themselves or failed to communicate personal limits, then you might struggle with boundary-setting later in life.

The behaviours you witnessed as a child or in early professional environments may have taught you to disregard your own needs, leading to feelings of guilt or discomfort when attempting to assert boundaries. That is particularly so when role models dismiss or disrespect boundaries, as those experiences can reinforce the belief that boundaries are unimportant or to be feared. That was my childhood.

Chapter 2: The Ripple Effect of Boundaries

Recognising the impact of positive and negative role models is critical in understanding how you set your boundaries. By reflecting on these influences, you can work to adopt healthy boundary practices while distancing yourself from any negative patterns that may have been internalised.

How boundaries change over time

Boundaries are dynamic and evolve as we grow and experience new challenges. As we become more self-aware and better understand what matters to us, we reassess our personal and professional boundaries. For example, boundaries that once seemed rigid may become more flexible as we mature, while changes like new relationships, career shifts or increased responsibilities may require us to set firmer boundaries to protect our wellbeing.

Recent developments, such as digital technology, have blurred the lines between work and personal life, reshaping boundaries around work-life balance. As self-care and flexibility gain priority, people are reassessing how to manage their personal and professional lives. Chapters Ten, Eleven and Twelve will examine in greater detail these changes, exploring how personal growth, shifting circumstances and societal changes influence the boundaries we establish.

Boundary violations are a human issue

Boundary violations aren't limited to interactions between genders — both men and women can be negligent of each other's boundaries. Workplace dynamics, friendships and power imbalances all influence how boundaries are respected or overlooked. Strong relationships foster clearer boundaries, as mutual respect encourages open conversations about personal comfort levels. However, familiarity can also lead to assumptions, making it essential to check in and ensure boundaries are upheld. Being mindful of how we interact, regardless of gender, helps create a culture of respect where everyone feels valued, heard and safe to set limits without fear of judgment or dismissal. See Chapter Five for insights on the various boundaries we set and how they can be crossed.

You are not your parents

As you reflect on your resilience and the origins of your boundaries, consider how your upbringing affected you and its effects on your current behaviour. For example, if you are a parent, how does the way you were raised impact how you raise your children? I want to be clear that this reflection is not about criticising anyone's parenting styles; we all do our best with the knowledge we have.

Many, if not most, people had no clear manuals or guidelines for parenting. Most of us learn through trial and error, relying on our own upbringing and life experiences. While resources for parenting are now more accessible, our personal experience can still have a lasting impact on how we parent our own children.

Our past experiences, whether positive or negative, influence our behaviour and decision-making in ways we often don't consciously recognise. This can have unintended consequences for our children. Words attributed to Carl Jung are applicable here. 'Until you make the unconscious conscious, it will rule your life and you will call it fate.'

Parenting styles, which vary in warmth, control and responsiveness, have been studied for their impact on children's development. Psychiatrist Daniel Amen referenced a University of Oregon study of 10,000 families, which found that permissive parenting — even with love — can lead to more mental health issues in children than firm, boundary-setting parenting. [11,12]

The study looked at four types of parents: permissive and hostile, permissive and loving, firm and hostile, and firm and loving. Amen noted that permissive and loving parents are linked to more mental health challenges in children than firm and hostile parents. He stressed the importance of boundaries in reducing anxiety and promoting healthy development.

> **Permissive and loving parents are linked to more mental health challenges in children.**

Authoritative parenting — a balance of warmth, responsiveness and appropriate control — leads to the best outcomes, including greater self-esteem and emotional regulation. In contrast, authoritarian parenting causes fear and low self-esteem, while permissive parenting leads to impulsivity and poor self-discipline. This shows the importance of balanced, boundary-setting parenting for healthy child development.

If you feel your parenting style may be affecting your children negatively, seek professional help. I found immense value in getting support for my traumas and parenting methods. With guidance, I was able to identify and mitigate areas where my parenting was lacking. Seeking help can make a significant difference in creating a healthier family environment. You'll find resources that can be useful in assisting with your parenting style in Appendix 2.

Recognising how boundaries help or hurt

Positive boundaries are essential for maintaining balance and empowering us to say 'no' when necessary while ensuring our personal needs are met. They help prevent exploitation or overextending ourselves in both personal and professional settings. On the other hand, weak or unclear boundaries may cause confusion or lead to people crossing our lines, resulting in emotional strain or a lack of respect from others.

Chapters Five and Six explore why boundaries may be both helpful and harmful, how personal beliefs, cultural expectations and past experiences shape our boundaries, and how to fine-tune them for better outcomes.

Overcoming guilt

I have struggled with guilt all my life. I am slowly learning to consider its impact on my health and wellbeing. Growing up as a people pleaser, I would say yes and take on too much without thinking about how it affected me. This taught others to rely on me for everything, and I felt responsible if things went wrong. A few years ago, I heard the actor Will Smith say, 'The road to power is in taking responsibility.'[13] This phrase has stuck with me, reminding me not to let others' lack of responsibility become my burden. It helps me set boundaries with reduced guilt and prioritise my wellbeing. That doesn't mean you should say no to everything. I encourage you to weigh what you agree to and understand the costs of not enforcing your boundaries.

Here are three factors I now consider (as a minimum) to help me reduce guilt when setting boundaries.

Acknowledging the importance of setting and maintaining boundaries

Consistently overextending yourself without setting proper boundaries can lead to burnout, stress and other health issues. Research from the American Psychological Association (APA)[14,15] highlights that chronic stress is linked to conditions such as anxiety, depression and cardiovascular disease.

Considering the impact on family and friends

Overcommitting can leave you less time and energy for family and friends, straining relationships. By setting boundaries, you ensure you have time for these important connections. In my previous book, *Break Free*, I discussed how guilt affected my relationships with my ex-husbands and daughters.[16] The fate of those relationships is why I have learnt to relinquish guilt and embrace saying no when necessary.

Understanding the career penalty

With loose or limited boundaries, you might take on too much, hurting the quality of your work and lowering your job performance. The result may slow your career growth and lead to job dissatisfaction or even quitting. I experienced this several times before realising that the path to less guilt was to put myself first.

The hidden effects of boundary crossing on those we love

We know, then, that boundaries impact personal wellbeing and significantly affect those around you, particularly in caregiving or parental roles. When parents' actions and behaviour hinder their children's autonomy — whether by setting unrealistic expectations, having no boundaries or being inconsistent in their approach — it can lead to confusion, stress and insecurity for the children.

Conversely, overly rigid boundaries can create emotional distance, leading to feelings of isolation and disengagement. Balancing clear, consistent boundaries with flexibility is crucial for fostering healthy relationships and supporting children's emotional development.

The consequences of boundary crossing on friends and family can be serious, affecting both individuals and their relationships. The impact may be lasting, but the consequences are not always visible. Here are some potential impacts.

Chapter 2: The Ripple Effect of Boundaries

Loss of trust and respect

Boundary violations can weaken trust and respect in relationships. When someone crosses another's boundaries, it can lead to feelings of betrayal and resentment, making it hard to rebuild trust. Depending on how often and how seriously boundaries are crossed, the relationship may even break down completely, causing grief for everyone involved.

Emotional distress

Boundary violations often cause emotional distress for the person affected and their friends and family. These violations can trigger emotions like anger, sadness or trauma, depending on the situation. For instance, if a family member is constantly criticised and belittled, they may feel degraded and worthless. This ongoing behaviour can harm mental wellbeing and strain family relationships. It may also affect bystanders who may feel powerless to intervene due to concerns for their safety and wellbeing.

Recent data from the Australian Institute of Health and Welfare shows that anxiety disorders are the leading issue for young women aged 15-24, making up 17% of their overall health burden.[17] In comparison, suicide and self-harm are the top concerns for young men at 12%. The National Study of Mental Health and Wellbeing also found that from 2020 to 2022, 26% of people aged 16-24 experienced high psychological distress, with young women (34%) being more affected than young men (18%).[18]

These statistics emphasise the heightened sensitivities required when navigating social behaviours for young women, who may experience increased anxiety as a result of social conditioning. Additionally, the impact of having their boundaries crossed can exacerbate these challenges, leading to significant emotional and psychological consequences.

Communication breakdown

Boundary violations can disrupt communication in relationships, causing avoidance, conflict or even a breakdown in communication. This is especially harmful in male-dominated industries, where poor communication can negatively affect women's mental health.

A 2023 report from the Australian Bureau of Statistics shows that about 39% of young Australians aged 16-24 experienced a mental disorder between 2020 and 2022, with young women being more affected. [19] As many of these young people will soon enter the workforce, bringing with them higher rates of anxiety and distress, these findings highlight the critical need for workplaces to foster effective and respectful communication practices to create supportive and inclusive environments.

Resentment and distance

Crossing boundaries can cause resentment and create distance between friends or family. The person whose boundaries were crossed may feel angry, while the one who crossed them might feel guilty or ashamed. This can create a divide, potentially leading to the relationship breaking down over time.

Impact on self-esteem

Crossing someone's boundaries can harm their self-esteem and self-worth. It may lead them to doubt their value, feel powerless or invalidated and struggle with shame or inadequacy. Lowered confidence can make it harder for them to assert their boundaries in the future.

Understanding the ripple effect

As we conclude this chapter on the ripple effect of boundaries, reflect on how your boundaries impact your wellbeing and those around you. How we set and maintain boundaries doesn't just affect our personal lives — it influences everyone with whom we interact, whether at home, at work or other areas of life. To better understand whether your boundaries are serving your needs and promoting the wellbeing of others, consider the following questions. These will help you align your actions with your values and refine your approach to boundary-setting, ultimately creating healthier relationships.

Guiding questions

1. How do the people around me feel about the boundaries I have set? Have I noticed any signs of frustration, stress or discomfort from them?

2. Have I clearly communicated my boundaries? Have I actively sought feedback on how they affect others?

3. Do I make space for others to express their feelings about my boundaries, and am I open to adjusting them when needed?

4. Are my boundaries rigid, or am I able to be flexible while still respecting my own needs and the needs of others?

5. Do I regularly reflect on whether my boundaries are too strict or causing unintended harm?

Resilience and Grit

*It is not what happens to you, but how
you react to it that matters.*

— Epictetus

When faced with challenges, two key qualities help us establish strong boundaries and stick to our values. Academic and author Angela Duckworth says resilience and grit are integral to long-term success. In her book *Grit: Why Passion and Resilience are the Secrets to Success,* she defines grit as the ability to persevere through challenges, maintain focus on your goals and push forward despite setbacks.[20] Resilience, a key component of grit, is the ability to bounce back from setbacks and stay motivated over time. I highly recommend Duckworth's book, as it provides powerful insights into cultivating and applying these traits to personal and professional growth.

Building on Duckworth's insights, it is clear that grit and resilience are essential for developing healthy boundaries. Grit keeps you committed to your goals, while resilience helps you uphold your boundaries in personal and professional relationships. Maintaining these boundaries requires the perseverance Duckworth describes, ensuring your values and wellbeing are protected, even when faced with challenges.

Your boundaries adapt as life changes — whether through new experiences, jobs or relationships. For example, the boundaries you set as a young professional might change when balancing work, family or health later in life. Adjusting boundaries helps maintain balance and strengthens the grit and resilience necessary to face life's challenges confidently.

In *The Anxious Generation,* social psychologist Jonathan Haidt highlights the rising anxiety levels among Generation Z, linking it to the rapid development of technology and the impact of social media.[21] He explains that constant comparisons to idealised online lives harm self-esteem and increase feelings of inadequacy. Smartphones were introduced in 2008, so many Generation Z children were raised with them and started using them before their brains were emotionally ready. Therefore, they are more likely to struggle with building resilience, a key skill for setting and maintaining boundaries.

Haidt writes that social media promotes superficial connections and instant gratification, which detract from real-life experiences needed to develop resilience. That makes it harder for Gen Z to assert themselves and protect their wellbeing, as they often compromise their boundaries due to online pressures. Social media amplifies external pressures, making it even more difficult for them to establish and uphold healthy boundaries.

Evolving grit and resilience

Grit and resilience have evolved across generations, particularly among women. Claudia Goldin, the 2023 Nobel Prize winner in Economics, researched gender inequality. Her book *Career and Family* outlines the women's century-long journey to equity.[22] She highlights that earlier generations faced different societal expectations, economic conditions and social barriers, which shaped their development of these traits differently from women today.

For women of past generations, grit and resilience were often born out of necessity. In the early to mid-20th century, they navigated male-dominated workplaces with few career opportunities, balancing work and home life with little support. Facing discrimination and societal expectations, they developed resilience to create opportunities and push for change. It was the foundation of the women's rights movements of the 1960s and 1970s, which fought for gender equality and workplace rights.

While gender equality has improved, modern challenges like social media, constant connectivity and balancing career with personal life require a new form of grit. Women must develop resilience against psychological pressures from unrealistic standards and societal comparisons. With the growing focus on mental health, the concepts of self-care and boundary-setting are now more accepted. However, today's challenges are often more about navigating complexities than the survival-driven grit of previous generations.

While grit and resilience may look different today, the need for these traits remains the same. Earlier generations built grit by facing societal obstacles, while modern women developed resilience by handling the psychological pressures of today's world. Each generation's challenges shape how they develop and show their grit and resilience.

A PERSONAL PERSPECTIVE

Looking back on my life, I am reminded of how my lack of boundaries when I was younger shaped my experiences. Now, instead of focusing on missed opportunities, I concentrate on the lessons I have learned. When things do not go as planned, I look for the positives or the lessons behind them. Resilience and grit have helped me navigate life's difficulties. However, I did not always have this mindset. Through facing challenges and setbacks, I have come to understand the importance of resilience and grit, not just for surviving but for growing stronger with each experience.

In 2015, after deciding to leave the military, I applied for a role with the Civil Aviation Safety Authority (CASA). Confident in my aviation knowledge, I was sure the job was mine, especially after progressing through three rounds of interviews. So, when they chose another candidate, I was deeply disappointed. Initially, I questioned my qualifications and the entire process. However, instead of dwelling on it, I asked myself, 'What can I learn from this? What feedback can I seek?' I realised I had been playing it

Chapter 3: Resilience and Grit

> *safe, sticking to roles I knew I could do and not pushing myself to grow.*
>
> *Reflecting on this setback, I began to see it as a blessing. Had I gotten that role, I would not have met my current husband (my biggest supporter), nor would I have been able to help others with their careers, which brings me great fulfilment. I understood that staying within my old boundaries would have limited my growth and experiences.*
>
> *This experience taught me the value of resilience and grit. I learned to reflect on my boundaries and the expectations I set for myself. Boundaries should grow with me as I adapt to new opportunities instead of holding back. This process of reflection and growth has been key in helping me build resilience, turning setbacks into opportunities for future success.*

Cultivating resilience for sustained success

Resilience is core to maintaining boundaries and achieving long-term success. As you read this book, I encourage you to consider the four pillars in Figure 1. I recommend these to clients when they face difficulties setting or maintaining boundaries.

> **Resilience is core to maintaining boundaries and achieving long-term success.**

Figure 1: Four pillars for cultivating resilience

Develop a growth mindset — This well-recognised principle was identified by Stanford professor Carol Dweck.[23] A growth mindset describes the belief that abilities and intelligence can be developed through dedication, effort and learning from mistakes. This approach helps you stay flexible and resilient when facing setbacks or challenges to your boundaries.

Surround yourself with supportive people (colleagues, mentors and friends) who can offer encouragement, especially when you feel your boundaries have been crossed. Chapter Twelve has strategies if you're lacking a support network.

Practice self-care — Physical and mental health is often neglected when boundaries are weak. Regular exercise, healthy eating and mindfulness can greatly boost resilience.

Chapter 3: Resilience and Grit

Set realistic goals — Don't try to do everything at once. This final step locks the pillars into a solid structure. Chapter Ten discusses the importance of setting realistic goals and breaking them into smaller steps so you can track progress and stay motivated. Regularly assess and adjust your boundaries to stay empowered.

> **Regularly assess and adjust your boundaries to stay empowered.**

You can maintain balance and success in your career by adapting them to changing situations, reviewing them often and bouncing back after setbacks. Embrace resilience and the art of possibility to support your ongoing progress. Remember, strong boundaries require constant attention and self-awareness.

Guiding questions

Building resilience and grit starts with self-reflection, as understanding your strengths, challenges and resources is key to navigating life's difficulties. Consider the following questions to uncover areas for growth and strategies for perseverance:

1. What previous challenges have you faced, and how did you overcome them? Reflect on past experiences to identify strengths and strategies that worked before.

2. How do you respond to setbacks or failures, and what can you learn from them? Examine your reactions to adversity to shift focus from obstacles to opportunities for growth.

3. What are your long-term goals, and how can you stay committed despite difficulties? Clarify your purpose to maintain motivation and perseverance when challenges arise.

4. Who can you turn to for support or guidance when you face tough situations? Build a strong support network to foster resilience by ensuring you don't face struggles alone.

5. How do you prioritise self-care and manage stress in your daily life? Resilience depends on maintaining physical and emotional health through activities that recharge and sustain you.

Throughout this book, I emphasise resilience and grit as the foundation for setting and maintaining boundaries. These traits will help ensure your boundaries are respected.

Navigating Societal Expectations

Boundaries are part of self-care. They are healthy, normal and necessary.

— DOREEN VIRTUE [24]

Women face many external pressures impacting their wellbeing, self-esteem and self-worth. These pressures come from gendered communication, beauty standards, workplace dynamics and cultural, religious and family obligations. All shape how women see themselves and live their lives.

In a world filled with societal norms and gender stereotypes, women often struggle to balance these expectations with their own needs. This pressure can lead to boundary violations that affect their independence and wellbeing. This chapter explores women's challenges in setting and maintaining boundaries amidst these pressures, offering insights and strategies to navigate them effectively. Before we proceed, it is essential to understand societal dynamics surrounding equality, equity and social justice.

Equality, equity and social justice

Equality and equity are often subjects of debate in workplace dynamics, especially in identifying and enforcing boundaries. Despite their frequent interchangeability, equality and equity are not the same. Each concept holds unique meanings and implications. Their subtle differences highlight a critical distinction that is not universally understood yet significantly affects the workplace environment. Some people even argue that equity and inclusion policies have swung too far, potentially leading to discrimination against men in efforts to increase female representation in the workplace. We're seeing that debate loudly in play in the USA in 2025.

Equality refers to treating everyone the same regardless of individual differences or circumstances. In the context of workplace boundaries, equality might mean applying the same rules or standards to all employees without considering their unique needs or circumstances. While equality is important for ensuring fairness and preventing discrimination, it may not always address underlying disparities or meet the specific needs of individuals. Figure 2 illustrates the differences.

Chapter 4: Navigating Societal Expectations

Figure 2: Equality, equity and social justice[25]

Equity, however, involves identifying and addressing individual differences to ensure fairness and opportunity for all. In terms of work boundaries, equity might involve acknowledging that employees have different personal boundaries or needs based on factors such as cultural background, personality or life circumstances. It requires considering these differences and adjusting policies, practices or support mechanisms accordingly to accommodate diverse needs and ensure everyone has the same access to resources and opportunities.

When it comes to boundaries at work, an equitable approach means recognising and respecting the diverse boundaries of employees to foster an inclusive and supportive environment. This topic is delicate because, even though the rational benefits are clear, many employees struggle to express their feelings about equity, equality and justice. Not everyone feels psychologically safe to share their true experiences. We must bring everyone on this journey to avoid fragmenting the organisation or creating marginalised groups.

> Women are expected to readily handle constant challenges to their boundaries.

Social justice involves ensuring a fair and impartial allocation of resources, opportunities and rights across society (or within the workplace) to address systemic disparities and foster inclusivity and fairness for everyone. In workplace boundaries, we must uphold the principles of social justice in their implementation and enforcement. That requires acknowledging and rectifying power imbalances, systemic biases and structural barriers that impede individual ability to establish and maintain boundaries effectively.

Chapter 4: Navigating Societal Expectations

Knowing what society expects

Almost a century after women's emancipation and decades after the women's liberation movement, societal expectations of women are still tied to gender roles that pressure them to focus on supporting others, their appearance and self-sacrifice. Women are expected to readily handle constant challenges to their boundaries. These expectations are unrealistic and unfair, as they force women to balance being assertive with societal norms that discourage confrontation.

Women are often judged harshly for their appearance and communication and are expected to balance caregiving while pursuing careers. In male-dominated professional environments, they may feel pressure to work harder to prove themselves, stay likeable and avoid being too assertive. These expectations add to the pressures that affect their personal and professional lives, limiting their opportunities and influencing how they handle their careers, relationships and identity.

Many women feel pressured to conform, suppressing their true selves to fit into gender roles that emphasise nurturing, selflessness and perfection. This constant masking erodes authenticity, leading to burnout, anxiety and a diminished sense of self-worth. Over time, this impacts relationships, careers and overall wellbeing, causing women to lose sight of their true needs and boundaries.

Navigating external influences

Alongside societal expectations, many factors affect a woman's ability to maintain boundaries. We'll explore workplace dynamics, gender bias and personal and professional relationships in later chapters.

Yet there are other damaging influences, including how women are portrayed in the media, various cultural, religious and family pressures, beauty standards, body autonomy and the lack of mutual support among women in the workplace. Understanding these influences is critical to building resilience and strategies to maintain boundaries confidently. Let's start with the media.

Chapter 4: Navigating Societal Expectations

The influence of media

The media influences perceptions of beauty, success and social norms, creating unrealistic expectations. Understanding the power and impact of those influences is vital to maintaining self-respect and healthy relationships.

It's more than the images of 'female perfection' that constantly fill our screens. Too often, it gets personal when a social media troll comments negatively on your size or what you're wearing when you post a picture of yourself with friends. If this happens often enough, you might start feeling bad about yourself and resort to extreme dieting or over-exercising to fit the unrealistic standards seen in magazines and online. These responses perpetuate unhealthy patterns and reinforce the original boundary violation when you neglected to assert your worth and individuality.

While researching this book, I found a social media report highlighting unethical media behaviour targeting women in leadership roles.[26]

In January 2024, Georgie Purcell, the youngest woman in Australia's Victoria State Parliament, was at the centre of controversy when a media outlet altered images of her, enlarging her breasts and dressing her in a midriff tank top to demean her. Ms Purcell confronted the media, which led to an apology. She pointed out that such treatment would not happen to a male MP, showcasing the unequal treatment women in public roles face.

This incident demonstrates how the media can victimise and distort images of women to sensationalise stories, crossing ethical boundaries and perpetuating the victimisation of women in positions of authority.

Another female leader, Jacinda Ardern, stands out for enduring much criticism during her time in office as Prime Minister of New Zealand. Most notably, much of the critique revolved around her appearance, perceived lack of experience and reactions to her pregnancy after she was elected.

Investigative reporter Anusha Bradley noted the troubling rise in misogyny and violence aimed at Jacinda Ardern before she resigned from public office.[27] The language used to describe Ardern became more violent, vulgar and repetitive, trying to dehumanise her and send a message that women like her are worthless and hated. The targeting of Ardern, as both a woman and a leader, is part of a broader pattern affecting all women with similar roles. Sadly, this rise in misogyny is happening worldwide.

The Reykjavik Index for Leadership tracks opinions on whether men or women are better suited to leadership.[28] The report aims to promote gender equality and diverse leadership, showing how leadership traits like decisiveness and assertiveness are judged differently based on gender. It highlights the biases and challenges women face in advancing their careers, noting that factors such as appearance are often used to judge women's leadership, while confidence is used to rate men's abilities.

The key message is that societal biases unfairly affect how women leaders are perceived and limit their career growth.

Chapter 4: Navigating Societal Expectations

Cultural, religious and family dynamics

Navigating cultural, religious and family dynamics around women's autonomy and boundaries can be difficult, as these outside influences heavily impact their wellbeing. In many contexts, societal norms and traditions limit women's roles and decision-making power, pressuring them to conform. These pressures often conflict with women's personal desires and boundaries, making it harder to assert their independence. The overlap of gender, ethnicity and faith adds complexity and highlights the need to understand how these external influences shape boundaries and affect women's wellbeing.

While I have been fortunate not to experience much of this type of external pressure, as a coach, I have seen many women from diverse backgrounds face significant challenges. Cultural, racial or religious traditions often lead to autonomy and boundaries overlooked in favour of family expectations. In these situations, women often feel pressured to conform to their families' wishes, sacrificing their personal values and beliefs. These practices can leave women disempowered and without control over their decisions.

CASE STUDY: BRIDGING TRADITIONS

Gurbinder is an Australian-born Indian engineer whose Hindu parents value arranged marriages. Her parents pressured her to marry a suitable Indian man who shared their Hindu faith. Gurbinder found herself at odds with them when she fell in love

> *with Ravi, a Muslim man from Bangladesh who migrated to Australia when he was young.*
>
> *As she navigated the complex dynamics of culture and religion, the situation challenged Gurbinder's independence and personal boundaries. Despite the traditional norms of her parents' generation dictating her role and behaviour, Gurbinder bravely went against their wishes and pursued a relationship with Ravi. Through coaching, she learned to respectfully communicate her feelings to her parents, advocating for her values while acknowledging their concerns. Ultimately, Gurbinder's courageous stand led her parents to accept her relationship with Ravi.*

This real example highlights the importance of understanding how external influences shape women's boundaries and impact their wellbeing in diverse cultural contexts.

Beauty standards and body autonomy

Women face societal conventions around beauty, which can affect their boundaries and body autonomy. Navigating these pressures is challenging and impacts more than just physical wellbeing. Unrealistic beauty standards can pressure women to conform. Subtle messages in advertisements or comments from peers and family shape how women view their bodies and impact feelings of self-worth. When these expectations intersect with race, ethnicity and gender identity, the relationship between women and their bodies becomes even more complex. Understanding the negative impact of these pressures is vital in recognising the broader effects on women's health, wellbeing and empowerment.

Figure 3: 'Cruel Culture' by Malcolm Evans, published Jan 6 2011. Reproduced with permission

Appearance

Unrealistic standards of external beauty pressure women to conform to certain body types, skin tones and features. This pressure can harm physical and mental health, causing women to blur their boundaries by prioritising appearance over wellbeing.

For example, some women resort to extreme dieting or cosmetic procedures to fit these ideals, even at the expense of their health. These practices can lead to mental health issues like eating disorders, body dysmorphia, anxiety and depression. Restrictive diets and cosmetic procedures may worsen body image concerns, contributing to low self-esteem and emotional struggles, and ultimately harming overall wellbeing.

As women age, they tend to become more self-accepting, with many embracing their authentic selves. A 2022 survey revealed that 72% of women believe media and advertising heavily influence beauty standards, while 49% say these norms also stem from observing other women. Around 20% of women attribute beauty standards to men. Interestingly, women over the age of fifty feel less pressure to conform to these standards, with many feeling more empowered to embrace their true selves as they age.[29]

Within the STEM community, I have noticed a positive shift emerging among younger women choosing comfort over fashion, such as wearing runners rather than uncomfortable stilettos in professional settings.

Objectification

Women are often judged based on their appearance rather than their abilities or character, leading to boundary violations like unwanted comments, catcalling or invasion of personal space. Many women have experienced walking down the street and receiving catcalls or disapproving looks based on their clothing and body shape.

Society makes broad assumptions and judgments based on appearance. That means dressing or acting in a way that invites objectification reinforces harmful stereotypes about women, even if doing so feels empowering to the woman. This highlights the complexity of personal boundaries, which vary from person to person.

Chapter 4: Navigating Societal Expectations

Self-worth tied to appearance

When a woman's value is tied to her appearance, it reinforces the idea that physical beauty is her most important attribute. This external focus on appearance can diminish her sense of worth when she struggles to meet often unattainable beauty standards.

Consequently, many women struggle to uphold their boundaries or advocate for themselves when their looks are judged or criticised. For example, you may have felt inadequate or had low self-esteem when you were growing up because you did not fit the narrow beauty ideals portrayed in the media and popular culture.

Pressure to conform

Women also face pressure to meet beauty standards at work, in social settings and on social media. This constant pressure can lead to self-monitoring, making it difficult for women to set boundaries around their appearance and personal space.

For example, some women have felt the need to spend time and money on beauty products to fit in with their social circle, even when doing so caused financial and emotional strain. We feel less pressured as we age, but these expectations still affect younger generations.

A PERSONAL PERSPECTIVE

My growing years were different from many young women, as I was shielded from the prevalent beauty standards that often weigh heavily on young girls. Unlike many of my peers, I did not have prominent female role models or friends who influenced my perception of hair, makeup and fashion. My father's stance against cosmetics and our limited financial resources kept me away from the world of beauty products. Additionally, the absence of social media during my upbringing spared me from continual bombardment with unrealistic ideals. While teen and beauty magazines still had some influence, it was not a daily occurrence for me.

Joining the military in my early twenties subjected me to reinforced expectations regarding appearance, with strict regulations limiting practices like wearing jewellery, makeup or extreme hairstyles. I noticed that some women rebelled when they were off-duty, changing to conform more to fashion. While I am not entirely immune to current beauty regimes, ingrained norms prevented me from conforming to such standards when I was younger. That experience made me an interested observer of the pressures on women in broader society.

Perceived beauty standards can also violate intellectual boundaries when women receive messages that their appearance is more important than their intelligence. Suggestions that beauty and intelligence cannot coexist imply that a beautiful woman may not be smart. Comments like 'With your looks, you can succeed anywhere'. Or 'You have brains and beauty — we better watch out!' are common in workplaces. These remarks may seem harmless but reflect biases that undervalue women's intellect. Women are capable, regardless of their appearance.

Chapter 4: Navigating Societal Expectations

Recognising workplace dynamics

Workplace dynamics often mirror societal expectations, influencing perceptions, behaviours and opportunities, particularly for women balancing professional competence with traditional gender norms. Gender biases and unequal power dynamics often lead us to doubt our skills and worth. Subtle biases, lack of recognition or limited opportunities can weaken confidence and create self-doubt.

Workplace dynamics can add further complexities depending on the type of STEM industry — whether in high-reliability or safety-critical industries like aviation, rail or defence or other areas like academia conducting research and development or teaching.

> Women face a double bind.

In these environments, organisational culture plays a significant role. Whether the culture is collaborative or competitive, hierarchical or flat, open or siloed, these dynamics can heighten the pressure to conform, complicate communication and affect the ability to assert personal limits. The varying expectations across industries and organisational structures can make setting and enforcing boundaries even more challenging, amplifying the impact of gender biases and creating additional barriers to personal and professional growth.

Gendered communications

The term 'gendered communication' refers to how people express themselves according to societal gender expectations. Shaped by upbringing and societal norms, these expectations impact women's experiences and can infringe upon their boundaries in social settings. This is a topic I will explore further in my PhD studies.

> Navigating gendered communication while maintaining boundaries is difficult.

The way a woman communicates, including her tone and demeanour, is often unfairly judged based on gender stereotypes. Women face a double bind: if we are assertive and confident, we risk being seen as aggressive or bossy; if we use a softer tone, we may be perceived as weak or lacking leadership. That makes it harder for women to communicate effectively and maintain boundaries at work, as we must balance assertiveness with approachability. Another challenge is that women and men use language differently; 'please' and 'thank you' may be seen as politeness from women, but interpreted as commands from men. Language differences can reinforce unequal power dynamics and affect women's boundaries in communication.

Gender differences in communication styles, particularly the tendency for women to use more nurturing language, are widely recognised in research.[30,31,32] Generally, women are socialised to communicate in ways that foster collaboration, empathy and inclusivity. That includes validating others' contributions, encouraging input and using language that builds rapport and fosters group cohesion. These traits can be interpreted as a lack of assertiveness in the workplace, especially in male-dominated industries.

In STEM fields, where women are often in the minority, these communication patterns might interact with gendered expectations and cultural norms. For instance, women in STEM might feel pressured to balance their nurturing communication style with the need to assert themselves in highly competitive, sometimes hierarchical, environments.

Deborah Tannen is the author of many books and articles about how the language of everyday conversations affects relationships. She suggests that women's collaborative communication may be undervalued compared to the direct, assertive communication often expected of male professionals, leading to challenges in career advancement.[33, 34]

NAVIGATING NEURODIVERSITY

Neurodivergence, particularly in individuals with conditions such as ADHD or autism, can further modify communication styles.[35] For example, neurodivergent individuals might provide more detailed explanations, often over-explaining to ensure understanding, which might differ from neurotypical communication patterns. This trait is especially evident in individuals with autism, who may communicate in more literal and detailed terms, potentially missing the subtleties of social context.

Neurodivergence creates additional layers of complexity in communication, where the nurturing communication

> *style associated with gender and the more direct, detailed communication tendencies of neurodivergent individuals can coexist or conflict. For neurodivergent women in STEM, there may be a unique challenge in navigating both gendered expectations and the traits associated with their neurodivergence.*

Navigating gendered communications

In coaching, I have noticed many women downplaying their achievements by describing themselves as 'just a...'. For example, they say, 'I'm just a mother' or 'I'm just an engineer'. Men rarely do this. Women must stop diminishing their contributions with minimising language to fully embrace their value.

Reflecting on gendered communication and assertiveness, I was inspired by Anneli Blundell's book *The Gender Penalty*, which explores the challenges that women face in male-dominated environments.[36] Blundell highlights how assertiveness is perceived differently for men and women, with women often penalised for displaying traits associated with masculinity.

Cynthia Kay, from CK and CO Media Productions, suggests that women can be seen as more effective when they balance assertiveness with relational language that fosters collaboration and respect.[37] Navigating gendered communication while maintaining boundaries is difficult, especially in professional settings where societal expectations influence how women express themselves. For example, a woman working in a male-dominated industry might struggle with being assertive during meetings. She

Chapter 4: Navigating Societal Expectations

may be labelled as 'too aggressive' or 'bossy' if she speaks up with clear, confident statements. Despite these challenges, women must state their boundaries confidently to maintain respect and autonomy at work.

Women shift the understanding of gendered communication by clearly communicating expectations to male colleagues, seeking allies and advocating for others. They foster mutual respect and collaboration by pointing out disparities without alienating colleagues. Chapter Eight offers strategies to address these challenges and ensure boundaries are respected and contributions valued.

When faced with inappropriate behaviour, a woman can state her boundaries in social settings. If a male colleague or acquaintance makes unwelcome comments or invades her personal space, she can calmly and firmly express her discomfort and set clear limits, stating that the behaviour is unacceptable. I've listed some suggested responses in the following table. However, women must be mindful of how their communication is perceived and interpreted to handle workplace dynamics and challenge gender biases effectively.

Table 1: Suggestions for handling workplace dynamics

Situation	What to say
Unwelcome comments	I would appreciate it if you could keep the conversation respectful. I don't find that comment appropriate.
	That kind of comment makes me uncomfortable. I'd prefer you didn't talk about it.

Situation	What to say
Personal space invasion	You are standing too close. Please step back and respect my personal space.
	Could you please step back? I'm not comfortable with that level of closeness.
Unwanted touch or attention	I don't appreciate being touched without my consent. Please don't touch me.
	I'm not comfortable with that behaviour. Please stop it immediately.

Myths around women's assertiveness

There are many myths about women's assertiveness and how the media portrays them. The following are the six most common uncovered during my research.

Myth 1 — Women are naturally less assertive than men, leading to the false belief that they lack confidence for leadership roles. This myth ignores the fact that assertiveness is a skill anyone can develop. For example, a female CEO might be unfairly labelled pushy or aggressive when asserting herself in a meeting, reinforcing the idea that women should be less assertive at work.

Myth 2 — Assertive women are bossy or domineering, which undermines their authority. For instance, a female politician advocating for policy change might be criticised for being too assertive, while a man doing the same would be praised.

Myth 3 — Women should conform to traditional gender roles, valuing nurturing over assertiveness. This misbelief can make it difficult for women to assert themselves in public roles, as they may feel pressured to soften their communication. For example, a

Chapter 4: Navigating Societal Expectations

female executive might adopt a more passive style to avoid being seen as too aggressive.

Myth 4 — Assertive women are emotional or irrational, dismissing their actions as driven by emotions rather than logic. For instance, a female journalist might be seen as overly emotional when assertively questioning a tough interviewee.

Myth 5 — Assertive women are unlikeable, implying confidence makes them less approachable. This stereotype undermines women's credibility, as seen when a confident female business leader is unfairly labelled as difficult by male peers despite her effective leadership.

Myth 6 — Media portray women in leadership as competitive, undervaluing the collaboration they actually offer. For example, when two women vie for the same promotion, their teamwork might be misinterpreted as rivalry, reinforcing the idea of female competitiveness.

These myths about women's assertiveness and media portrayal reinforce harmful stereotypes and make it harder for women to assert themselves confidently. Despite this, women in public roles like Jacinda Ardern, Georgie Purcell and Julia Gillard show resilience and determination when facing media scrutiny. They defy stereotypes by proving their competence and strength. Some call out media boundary violations, pushing back against unfair treatment. By challenging

> Rigid gender roles and cultural norms can also make you feel guilty.

these myths and asserting themselves, women in leadership pave the way for greater gender equality and representation in leadership.

The impact of external pressures on wellbeing and self-worth

Society often promotes the idea that it is possible to excel in every area of life — such as being an athlete, executive, parent and individual all at once. However, achieving this balance is extremely difficult, and something usually has to give. Social media adds to the pressure by showing only the highlights of people's lives. Hiding their struggles reinforces unrealistic expectations, harms wellbeing, lowers self-worth and strains resilience, especially when the ideal of 'having it all' seems out of reach.

The pressure on women to excel simultaneously in work, social and home life can be overwhelming, often leading to stress, anxiety and eventually burnout — a state of emotional, mental and physical exhaustion resulting from prolonged and excessive stress. From my experience as a single parent raising two daughters while working in a male-dominated field without family support, I understand how these demands can erode resilience. Additionally (as we'll discuss in Chapter Eleven), the lack of digital boundaries exacerbates burnout by blurring the lines between personal and professional time, leaving little room for rest and recovery.

If you face similar challenges, you may internalise external pressures and tie your self-worth to meeting them. For example,

Chapter 4: Navigating Societal Expectations

the pressure to succeed in your career might lead you to sacrifice your mental wellbeing, increasing stress and lowering self-esteem. Rigid gender roles and cultural norms can also make you feel guilty when prioritising your needs over caregiving duties. These pressures can weaken resilience and boundary-setting efforts, as the constant push to meet unrealistic expectations makes it harder to uphold your limits. Over time, this erodes wellbeing and makes protecting personal and professional boundaries more challenging.

A PERSONAL PERSPECTIVE

While in the military, there was one instance when I reacted strongly to a boundary violation that significantly impacted my self-worth and wellbeing. I was meeting with my squadron flight support engineering officer about my request to be posted to sea. I wanted to get some operational sea time experience, which, in turn, would allow me to get promoted. I expected to discuss when this would be and which ship I would be posted to.

However, in response to my request for a sea posting, he asked, 'What would you do with your children if you were posted to sea?' This line of questioning took me aback, as I was sure my male counterparts were not asked this question if they had children. My immediate reaction was, 'What the heck do my children have anything to do with this?'

His question caught me off guard. Before I could process a response, my emotional brain took over. I felt a surge of anger bubbling up within me. It felt like a direct attack on my capabilities as a professional.

Despite my years of dedicated service, the specific training I had already undertaken to take on a sea posting and strong competence in my role, I suddenly felt reduced to nothing more than a caregiver, as if my worth in the military was solely determined by my ability to juggle parenting responsibilities. The question triggered a wave of frustration, leaving me questioning my value and competence in my military career and as a parent. However, I showed no visible emotion, as I wanted to be seen as capable and competent.

The impact of that boundary violation stayed with me long after the meeting concluded. I mentally replayed the encounter over and over, wrestling with feelings of inadequacy and frustration. It took considerable time and effort to rebuild my sense of self-worth and remind myself that someone else's narrow expectations did not dictate my value as a professional and a parent. This experience was a clear reminder of the importance of asserting my boundaries and challenging the societal norms that undermine autonomy and self-worth.

Interestingly, this incident motivated me to prove my competence and build resilience. It pushed me to pursue engineering studies and eventually return to the squadron as an engineering officer. While I never had the opportunity to serve at sea due to the challenges of being a woman in a male-dominated field at the time, the experience helped me grow in self-awareness and better understand my motivations.

Chapter 4: Navigating Societal Expectations

 Guiding questions

As we end this chapter, reflect on the following questions to establish and maintain healthy boundaries in various social settings:

1. What matters most to me? How can I establish boundaries that align with my values and priorities? How do I identify what is not so important to me?

2. Do I set limits on my time and energy? How can I become better at saying 'No' to requests or commitments that do not align with my priorities?

3. Do I trust my instincts when something feels uncomfortable or inappropriate? How can I assert my boundaries based on my intuition?

4. Do I surround myself with supportive individuals who respect my boundaries? How can I seek support from allies when needed?

5. Do I practice self-care to nurture my physical, emotional and mental wellbeing? How can I prioritise self-care practices to maintain strong boundaries?

Boundary Foundations

Daring to set boundaries is about having the courage to love ourselves, even when we risk disappointing others.
— BRENÉ BROWN[38]

Boundaries come from individual experiences, societal norms, cultural values and personal beliefs. Our early family interactions shape ideas about privacy, personal space and emotions, influencing how we manage boundaries in future relationships.

Individual experiences greatly influence how we set and tolerate boundaries. Interactions with parents, siblings, caregivers and peers shape our sense of safety, trust and vulnerability. Our boundaries should also evolve as we go through various stages of life, reflecting changes in our values, beliefs and priorities. Psychological factors, such as personality traits and emotional intelligence, further influence our boundary-setting behaviours, making each person's approach to boundaries unique.

Our values, beliefs and priorities guide how we set boundaries. As I explored in my earlier book, *Break Free*, they protect what matters most to us and help us decide which behaviours are acceptable in our interactions.[39] Ultimately, our boundaries are shaped by a mix of personal, relational, cultural and societal factors that influence how we manage relationships and interactions with others.

Elements of a boundary

My view of what makes a healthy boundary focuses on three key elements: respect, understanding and clarity. When these three overlap, a healthy boundary is formed. This model (Figure 4) forms the foundation for relationships based on trust, compassion and effective communication.

Chapter 5: Boundary Foundations

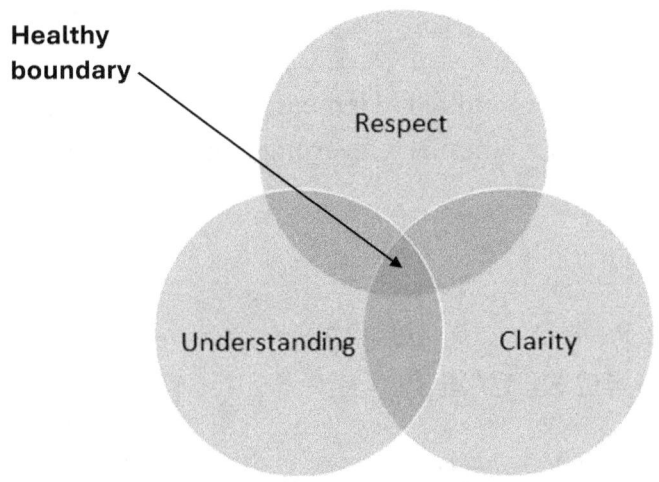

Figure 4: Elements of a healthy boundary

Respect means recognising and valuing each person's right to set boundaries without judgment. *Understanding* involves appreciating the reasons behind someone's boundaries and promoting active listening and empathy. *Clarity* is about clearly expressing your boundaries and expectations.

When respect and understanding come together, we communicate openly and empathetically, leading to cooperation rather than conflict. For example, when one person sets a boundary, the other's respect acknowledges it, and their understanding helps them grasp the reasons behind it. That creates a supportive environment where both individuals feel valued, fostering a healthy and stable relationship. It is important to acknowledge that external factors, like workplace rules, influence some boundaries.

People often interact as representatives of organisations, which can sometimes clash with their personal values. While this is beyond the boundary model described above, it is worth remembering when navigating boundaries.

We can see the three boundary elements in action with Samantha, who wanted to set a boundary regarding personal space with her colleague Alex.

> ## CASE STUDY: BOUNDARY-SETTING SUCCESS
>
> *Samantha felt Alex stood too close to her during conversations, so she approached him to express her concerns and to set a boundary regarding personal space. Alex listened attentively and asked how close was too close for her, recognising that comfort levels with personal space vary between individuals. Reflecting on his own experiences, he considered whether cultural differences or personal habits influenced his approach. Acknowledging Samantha's perspective, he assured her that he understood the importance of her personal space and promised to respect her boundaries in future. From then on, Alex consciously adjusted his behaviour to ensure Samantha felt comfortable. This open dialogue fostered mutual respect strengthening their professional relationship, and creating a more inclusive and considerate work environment.*

I've simplified the conversation between Samantha and Alex, but the point is that if you do not communicate that your boundary is being violated, you cannot be upset with the person who is unaware of it.

When Samantha communicated her boundaries, Alex's respect ensured he acknowledged and honoured her request. By understanding her reasons, he acknowledged the importance of her boundary, whether for personal comfort or on professional grounds. This blend of respect and understanding promoted open, empathetic communication, creating a cooperative work environment that strengthened their professional relationship.

When respect and clarity align, it encourages clear communication and consideration for each other's feelings, making both parties feel comfortable expressing their needs and fostering a supportive and collaborative workplace. This open communication strengthens mutual respect and enhances the health of their professional relationship. When understanding and clarity come together, boundaries are communicated with consideration for each other's feelings, building trust and respect.

Once we understand what a healthy boundary looks like, the next step is identifying the different types of boundaries and recognising how they can be violated.

Distinct types of boundaries

Nedra Glover Tawwab is an American mental health therapist and relationship expert. She identifies six key types of boundaries: intellectual, material, time, emotional, physical and sexual, in her book *Set Boundaries and Find Peace*.[40]

When researching this book, I discovered two further boundaries that significantly impact our lives. They are relational and digital boundaries. Together, these eight categories form the basis of personal boundaries, where we may be strong in some areas and weaker or lacking in others.

Boundary crossings, particularly in physical, emotional and professional interactions, are increasingly recognised as having widespread societal and individual impacts. Movements like #MeToo have illuminated the frequency and severity of violations, particularly among women, by exposing patterns of harassment, abuse and exploitation across industries.

Building on Tawwab's ideas, let's consider examples of how these boundaries might be violated at work and home. If you need a shortcut here, Chapter Nine provides valuable strategies for dealing with situations where another person is not respecting your boundaries.

Intellectual boundaries

> It is okay to have an opinion, but not okay to force it on others.

Intellectual boundaries involve respecting others' thoughts, ideas and opinions while staying true to your beliefs. These boundaries promote respectful conversations, allowing different perspectives without imposing your views on anyone else. It is okay to have an opinion, but not okay to force it on others. Intellectual boundaries ensure autonomy in thinking and decision-making, fostering open, constructive communication without belittling those who hold different views. Violations include dismissing someone's opinion without consideration,

Chapter 5: Boundary Foundations

interrupting or continually talking over them in discussions, sharing their ideas without permission and ignoring their specific area of expertise.

CASE STUDY: STRUGGLE WITH RESPECT AND RECOGNITION

Larissa, a graphic designer, found herself in a challenging situation at work. During a brainstorming session for an upcoming project, she shared what she thought was a groundbreaking idea, then noticed a senior colleague quickly dismissed it without thoughtful consideration or discussion.

In team meetings, Larissa was often interrupted and talked over, making it hard for her to contribute fully. Colleagues shared her ideas without her consent, sometimes with others taking credit for her work. These boundary violations undermined her expertise and eroded her sense of respect within the team. Larissa felt disheartened and undervalued. She began questioning her abilities, stifling her creative potential and hindering her professional growth.

To address the boundary violations she experienced, Larissa took the proactive step of documenting her ideas and sharing them via email before team meetings. By doing so, she created a clear record of her contributions, ensuring that her work was formally acknowledged and making it more difficult for others to take credit for her ideas without proper attribution. This action helped Larissa preserve ownership of her thoughts and set a professional tone for the team, reinforcing the importance of respecting intellectual contributions. She protected her expertise and regained her sense of value within the team.

Women's intellectual boundaries are often disrespected in the workplace when gender stereotypes portray women as less competent, leading to their ideas being undervalued or ignored.

> There is common confusion between confidence and competence.

There is common confusion between confidence and competence. When men appear confident, it can be taken as competence. Men are encouraged to appear confident regardless of their skill level. Those assumptions don't always apply to confident women, who are more likely to be seen as aggressive or bossy. These judgments reinforce stereotypes and diminish women's contributions, creating a culture where women's ideas are sidelined in favour of their male counterparts.

Power imbalances in workplace hierarchies can overshadow women's voices in decision-making. Workplaces emphasising assertiveness and competitiveness may also overlook women who communicate more collaboratively or thoughtfully.

Implicit bias is the unconscious attitudes or stereotypes that influence our actions and decisions. It frequently results in unintentional discrimination, reinforcing existing stereotypes and inequality. These biases affect how women's ideas are viewed, leading to harsher scrutiny or even crediting their ideas to others. Addressing implicit bias means challenging gender stereotypes, promoting inclusive leadership and creating work environments that value diverse perspectives. There's more on overcoming gender bias at work in Chapter Five.

Chapter 5: Boundary Foundations

A PERSONAL PERSPECTIVE

Like many women in STEM careers, I have faced numerous boundary violations, but one moment stands out. After leaving the military in 2017, I became a system safety engineering consultant in the rail industry. During a workshop on a train maintenance facility design, I was the only female participant among about twenty men from various areas of the rail environment, including engineers, maintenance staff and train operators.

Lacking confidence in the new domain, I opted to take the meeting minutes while a more experienced male colleague led the discussion. However, whenever I tried to ask questions, the men in the room often ignored or talked over me.

The turning point came during a break when the men started debating whether the role of maintenance worker or engineer was superior. I stepped in, asking a question that linked both roles, drawing from my background as an avionics technician turned engineer. This shifted their perception of me from a quiet note-taker to someone capable and knowledgeable. While I gained respect, it was frustrating that I had to again prove my technical skills to be treated as fairly as I should have been from the start.

The kind of behaviour I experienced in the story above is not uncommon in environments where male dominance is reinforced by historical and systemic gender biases. Research confirms that women in male-dominated fields often have to demonstrate their competence more overtly than their male counterparts to be respected.[41,42] Many women in male-dominated industries face challenges in earning respect and being taken seriously. Too often, I've seen women marginalised as their expertise is overlooked or dismissed — particularly when they are outnumbered by male colleagues. This dynamic is compounded by the tendency for women to be expected to prove their abilities, even if they are already qualified for the role. It is especially true when women are new to a domain and feel compelled to prove themselves through actions rather than words.

Material boundaries

Material boundaries refer to people's limits regarding possessions, resources and personal spaces like desks or bedrooms. These boundaries help protect personal belongings, financial resources and private spaces by setting clear expectations about borrowing, sharing and respecting property.

Violations of material boundaries might include borrowing items, entering someone's bedroom or workspace or going through others' belongings — all without permission. It also extends to leaving messes in shared spaces like living rooms, kitchens or other communal areas, disregarding the needs and comfort of others. Financial violations could involve a partner mismanaging shared finances or spending irresponsibly without considering joint bills.

CASE STUDY: CROSSING THE LINE IN SHARED LIVING

In a shared household of four, Sonia noticed her toiletries – shampoo, toothpaste and perfume – were frequently used by her housemate, Tina, without permission. Despite labelling her belongings and giving verbal reminders, Sonia was frustrated when her things were often used without consent. She also felt uncomfortable when Tina ignored her need for privacy by entering her bedroom without knocking. Housemate Lisa faced similar issues with Jane, who consistently neglected her cleaning duties and left the communal areas untidy. These material boundary violations created tension and discomfort, disrupting the harmony of the shared household.

Societal expectations often position women as primary caregivers, leading to assumptions that they should be more generous with their material possessions. This perspective is rooted in traditional gender roles that assign domestic and nurturing responsibilities predominantly to women. For instance, in Australia, women perform 50% more housework than men, a disparity that has remained unchanged for the last two decades.[43,44] This imbalance reflects persistent gender norms that not only burden women with additional unpaid labour.

The concept of 'mankeeping' is where women shoulder the emotional burdens of their male partners.[45] It reinforces societal norms that expect women to manage others' needs alongside their own. This expectation extends to material boundaries, as women's possessions and time are often seen as communal resources due to their caregiving roles. As a result, their personal space and belongings are more likely to be used without explicit consent, further diminishing their autonomy.

Additionally, existing power dynamics often favour men in areas like finances and decision-making, which can lead to men's needs being prioritised over women's.[46] For insights on dealing with these power dynamics, see Chapter Eight.

The risk of backlash

My perception is that women tend to negotiate less and set lower goals because they fear social backlash when they stand for themselves.

> Many women are taught early to put others first.

A 2021 study on gender differences in entitlement and apprehension highlighted how societal expectations and reactions make it difficult for women to set boundaries at work.[47] This backlash occurs because entitlement is often seen as a masculine trait, and assertive women risk being viewed negatively. Men's higher sense of entitlement, shaped by societal roles, worsens this gap.

Furthermore, cultural norms that value generosity and selflessness can pressure women to prioritise others' needs over their boundaries. Many women are taught early to put others first, leading them to downplay their boundaries to keep the peace. Additionally, a lack of education on healthy boundary-setting contributes to misunderstandings or disregard for women's boundaries.

Time boundaries

Time boundaries involve how people manage their time and availability, ensuring a balance between work, leisure, self-care and relationships. These boundaries help individuals prioritise commitments and avoid burnout by ensuring they have enough time to rest. This type of boundary violation includes constantly interrupting someone or demanding their time without respecting their need for focus or personal time. Another example is disregarding meeting times or deadlines, causing delays and disrupting productivity.

> **CASE STUDY: BALANCING WORK AND FAMILY RESPONSIBILITIES**
>
> *Megan, a program manager and mother of two school-aged children, balanced her work responsibilities with family commitments by working flexibly from home two days a week. She clearly communicated to her team that she was unavailable for meetings between 2:30 pm and 4:00 pm on the days she worked from home due to school pick-up duties. She said she would address work issues later in the evening, from 6:30 pm to 8:00 pm, but she did not expect her team to attend meetings then.*
>
> *Despite her company's agreement about her adjusted work hours, Megan's colleagues regularly scheduled meetings during her unavailable time. They justified this by stating their own non-*

> *work commitments, like sports or socialising, and suggesting that Megan rearrange her schedule or find someone else to do her role if she could not accommodate their meeting times.*

Megan's situation highlights the challenges that working parents face in balancing professional and personal lives. Her colleagues often disregarded her boundaries despite her efforts to communicate her availability and adjust her schedule. This example reminds us of the need for supportive work environments that respect all employees' commitments, regardless of gender or family status. It also shows the importance of understanding the unique challenges working mothers face and promoting gender equality and work-life balance. Megan's work after hours to compensate for time taken in the afternoon reflects a familiar pattern where women feel pressured to collaborate and please others to be seen as hardworking and high-performing.

The Australian Government has introduced industrial relations reforms to address time boundary violations, giving workers the right to ignore out-of-hours calls and emails without penalty. This law, effective from August 2024, states that it is unreasonable for employers to expect constant availability outside agreed work hours, as it affects work-life balance and personal time. Disregarding requests for personal time intrudes on privacy and hinders rest, highlighting the importance of respecting boundaries. Women often face added pressure due to traditional gender roles, with the assumption that they should be more accommodating with their time.

Chapter 5: Boundary Foundations

Emotional boundaries

Emotional boundaries protect your feelings and thoughts while respecting others. They help you set personal limits, express emotions appropriately and maintain emotional wellbeing. These boundaries are essential for healthy relationships, balancing empathy with self-care and preventing manipulation. Examples of emotional boundary violations include gaslighting, where someone manipulates your perception of reality, using guilt or fear to control your emotions, or dismissing and belittling your feelings and experiences.

> ### CASE STUDY: UNSEEN CHAINS
>
> *Cathy had been in a relationship with Mark for several months and things seemed to be going well. At least, that was what she thought. However, as time went on, she noticed subtle signs of emotional manipulation. Mark often made comments that left her questioning her thoughts and feelings. For example, when Cathy voiced her discomfort about a situation, Mark would brush off her concerns or accuse her of overreacting, leading her to question her feelings.*
>
> *He frequently used guilt trips, saying things like 'I've done so much for you, and this is how you treat me' to control her behaviour. When Cathy tried standing up for herself, Mark would downplay her emotions and tell her she was overreacting. For instance, 'you're overreacting again. I can't believe you are making a big deal out of this!' Cathy felt trapped and invalidated as her emotional boundaries were repeatedly crossed, leaving her confused, anxious and drained. Despite trying to address Mark's*

> *behaviour, he continued to manipulate her emotions, making her feel powerless. It was not until Cathy turned to friends and family for support that she saw the manipulation for what it was and started taking steps to protect her emotional wellbeing.*
>
> *Note: This case study has been simplified to illustrate the concept of emotional boundary crossings. It is important to recognise that emotional boundary violations can be complex and, in some cases, perceived as domestic abuse. While this book does not offer specific guidance on this issue, resources and organisations are available to support those experiencing such challenges. There's a list of relevant support networks at the end of this book in Appendix 3.*

As we've seen, women's emotional boundaries are often overlooked due to societal and cultural norms. These views have led to women being regarded as more emotionally available, making it easier for their boundaries to be ignored. Gender stereotypes label women as more emotional or sensitive, causing their boundaries to be dismissed.

Having absorbed messages about accommodating and avoiding conflict, women prioritise harmony over setting and holding boundaries. In the workplace, women may struggle to set emotional boundaries, especially in male-dominated environments that value assertiveness over emotional expression.

Women who assert their emotional boundaries may be unfairly viewed as too emotional or unprofessional, leading to backlash or discrimination. As a result, their emotional needs may be overlooked because they are less likely to speak up. Disrespect for women's emotional boundaries is often tied to long-standing gender norms, stereotypes and power dynamics in personal and professional relationships.

Relational boundaries

Relational boundaries define the expectations, limits and rules governing interactions within any relationship — personal or professional. These boundaries set the parameters for levels of intimacy, communication and acceptable behaviour, ensuring that individuals feel respected

> Women prioritise harmony over setting and holding boundaries.

and valued. Relational boundaries are often more flexible than emotional boundaries and evolve depending on the context of the relationship. When violated, relational boundaries lead to confusion, misunderstandings or a breakdown in respect, which may destabilise the relationship.

For example, in a professional setting, men and women may experience different relational boundaries regarding communication styles. Men are often more comfortable with direct and competitive interactions, while women might prioritise collaborative and supportive communication.[48]

A woman in a meeting where more dominant, assertive male colleagues overshadow her ideas might feel excluded from the decision-making process or disrespected because her contributions aren't given equal weight. In such a scenario, it is important to establish boundaries by asserting her right to speak up and have her input valued. These conversations are an opportunity to redefine how communication flows in the workplace and promote a more respectful and inclusive environment.

> ## NAVIGATING NEURODIVERSITY
>
> *It's worth noting that neurodivergent individuals often find it challenging to understand emotional and relational boundaries. That's because they process social cues, facial expressions and tone of voice differently. This can lead to unintentional boundary crossings or difficulty recognising when their own emotional boundaries are violated. For instance, they may struggle to identify manipulative behaviour or realise when they are being overly open.*
>
> *Clear communication and supportive environments help neurodivergent individuals understand and maintain emotional boundaries. This is especially relevant in STEM fields, where a higher proportion of people may exhibit traits of ADHD or autism. For further insights into communication styles and creating supportive environments for neurodivergent individuals, refer to Appendix 4, which lists recommended readings on the topic.*

Digital boundaries

Digital boundaries define how we engage with technology and manage our online presence, including the time we spend on devices, the information we share, and how we interact with others in digital spaces. When these boundaries are not upheld, they can lead to burnout, privacy violations and strained relationships. Overuse of technology encroaches on personal time, disrupting sleep or creating unnecessary stress while oversharing or unclear online expectations blur the lines between professional and personal life. Establishing and maintaining digital boundaries is essential for protecting your wellbeing and fostering balanced, healthy connections — online and offline. To learn strategies to maintain your boundaries in the digital era, refer to Chapter Eleven.

Physical boundaries

A physical boundary refers to personal space and comfort with touch, distance and intimacy. You've read an example in Lisa and Alex's conversation at the start of this chapter. Our upbringing and comfort levels shape how we feel about these things. These boundary violations can include unwanted physical contact or ignoring someone's discomfort. For example, continuing to touch someone after they have expressed discomfort, standing too close or imposing physical affection like hugs or kisses without consent.

CASE STUDY: OVERLY FAMILIAR

Gary, a senior manager at an engineering firm, often interacted with colleagues from various offices during meetings and gatherings. One day, upon encountering Jill, a female colleague from another office, Gary greeted her in what he perceived as a friendly and informal manner due to his culture and upbringing. Without hesitation, he moved in for a quick hug and a kiss on

> *the cheek, unaware that he was encroaching on Jill's personal space. Despite Gary's intentions of friendship and familiarity, his actions undermined Jill's sense of security and made her uncomfortable.*
>
> *Pressing such gestures onto someone without their explicit consent or in the absence of a pre-existing rapport can be deeply unsettling and intrusive. Whatever Gary's intent, his impact was that Jill felt her boundaries had been crossed.*

Lack of awareness of others' boundaries can lead to assumptions that women are more cooperative, making it easier for their personal space to be invaded. In male-dominated workplaces, women may feel pressured to tolerate boundary violations to avoid negative career impacts. This has been worsened by the normalisation of inappropriate behaviour. That is unwelcome behaviour that demeans, humiliates or intimidates an individual. It includes sexual harassment, verbal abuse and any form of discriminatory comments or actions based on race, gender, age, religion, or other protected characteristics, as well as the fear of speaking up.[49,50]

Physical violence (hitting or pushing) is a serious violation of personal boundaries and causes significant harm and trauma. While laws and workplace policies aim to prevent this, it still occurs. To address this, workplaces should raise awareness of unacceptable behaviour, enforce clear policies and challenge gender biases to ensure physical boundaries for all, especially women, are respected and upheld.

Chapter 5: Boundary Foundations

Sexual boundaries

Sexual boundaries define what is appropriate in intimate interactions, focusing on consent, personal autonomy and respect. Touching someone without consent or making comments about their sexual orientation or appearance that cause discomfort are clear violations. Sexual boundary violations can include unwanted advances, remarks or gestures that create an uncomfortable environment.

Any non-consensual sexual activity, such as unwanted touching or penetration, is a serious violation of autonomy. Using manipulation or threats to force sexual acts violates human rights and the law.[51] If such an event occurs, women must be able to safely rely on the reporting and accountability processes in their organisation.

Know the law

Many sexual boundaries are unspoken, but laws like the *Fair Work Act 2009* and *Fair Work Regulations 2009* clearly define unacceptable workplace behaviour. However, women often have to navigate a patriarchal culture that objectifies female bodies and highlights male desires, which can be amplified in professional settings where men hold authority. This creates power dynamics that may pressure women to tolerate inappropriate behaviour to protect their careers. Disrespect for women's sexual boundaries at work often stems from cultural norms, power imbalances and gender inequality, especially in male-dominated industries, manifesting through inappropriate touching, sexual innuendos and explicit jokes.

CASE STUDY: HOW WOMEN PRESENT THEMSELVES

Kristie, a young female scientist, faced the daunting task of navigating her workplace environment while constantly having to consider how she dressed, interacted and communicated. She worked in a patriarchal environment that created a constant threat to her sexual boundaries, as she had to constantly be on guard against unwanted advances, comments or behaviours from her male colleagues. The pressure to conform to societal expectations of femininity while maintaining professionalism added further complexity to Kristie's experience. She contended with fear of retaliation or professional repercussions if she spoke out against boundary violations, leading her to internalise her discomfort and endure instances of harassment or misconduct in silence.

Kristie's case highlights the widespread issue of sexual boundary violations in many workplaces and the difficulties women face in dealing with them. A lack of awareness about healthy relationships between men and women in diverse cultural settings can lead to misunderstandings around consent. Fear of retaliation or social backlash can make it harder for women to enforce their boundaries, as they may worry about being blamed or facing career consequences.

The concept of 'respectful autonomy' — the ability to make independent decisions about one's life, boundaries and wellbeing while respecting others' autonomy — is crucial to addressing women's challenges in advocating for themselves. In environments lacking education about consent and healthy boundaries, women often struggle to assert their needs, perpetuating power imbalances and disrespect. This highlights the need for a cultural shift to respect and uphold women's autonomy and sexual boundaries in all areas of life.

Guiding questions

To uncover areas where your boundary foundations may need strengthening, take a moment to reflect on the following questions.

1. Do I feel uncomfortable saying 'No' to others, even when it's necessary for my wellbeing?
2. Am I often overwhelmed by others' expectations of my time and energy?
3. Do I feel drained or resentful after helping others, even when I didn't want to?
4. Have I experienced guilt or anxiety when I prioritise my needs over those of others?
5. Do I tolerate disrespectful behaviour because I fear conflict or rejection?
6. Am I constantly apologising, even when I haven't done anything wrong?
7. Do I struggle to express my emotions, leading to emotional suppression?
8. Do I feel responsible for other people's happiness or wellbeing, even at my own expense?
9. Do I allow others to step too far into my personal space, either physically or emotionally?
10. Am I often stuck in toxic relationships because I don't set or enforce limits on others' behaviour?

Chapter 5: Boundary Foundations

Healthy boundaries are vital for wellbeing and self-respect. Poorly enforced boundaries can lead to resentment, burnout and emotional harm. Clear limits empower us to protect our energy, foster growth and build fulfilling relationships, ensuring a balanced, resilient and empowered life.

Just as a house without locks invites intruders, a life without boundaries opens the door to negative influences that can drain energy, hinder growth and damage relationships. Setting and protecting boundaries safeguards emotional wellbeing and empowers healthier, more fulfilling lives.

Trigger Points

*Human beings are not creatures of logic;
we are creatures of emotion. And we do not
care what is true. We care how it feels.*

— DALE CARNEGIE [52]

Do you know how your brain works? When exploring boundary violations, it is useful to understand how our emotional and logical brains interact.

The emotional brain, or limbic system, includes structures like the amygdala, hippocampus and hypothalamus, as shown in Figure 5.

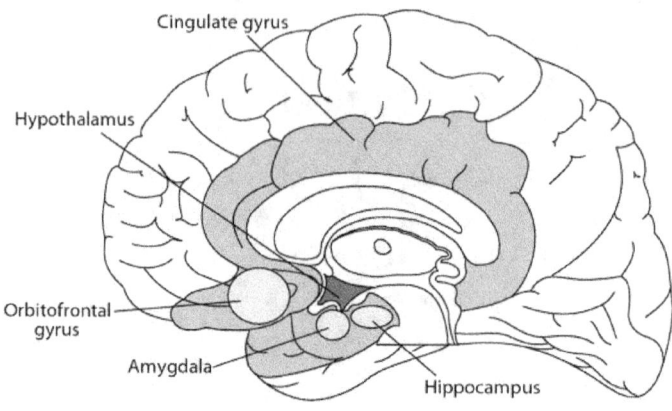

Figure 5: The limbic system[53]

It plays a crucial role in regulating emotions, memory, motivation and specific aspects of behaviour. The limbic system often operates beneath our conscious awareness, reacting instinctively to perceived threats to our boundaries and wellbeing.

Our subconscious responses impact behaviour and decision-making, often overpowering rational thought.

> **Resilience is core to maintaining boundaries and achieving long-term success.**

However, the logical brain (in the frontal lobe) may struggle to control emotional reactions, driving our response to boundary violations. Understanding how the emotional and logical brains interact offers insights that leave us better equipped to handle interactions.

Chapter 6: Trigger Points

Understanding your response to boundary violations

The 'chimp', or emotional brain, reacts impulsively and emotionally, explains Steve Peters in *The Chimp Paradox.*[54] This primitive part of the brain can lead to irrational behaviour, undermining our goals. He contrasts the chimp brain with the human brain (logical thinking) and stresses the importance of managing the emotional brain for personal growth and success.

Peters' book is insightful because it examines how the reactions of our emotional chimp brain often lead to adverse outcomes. For example, when faced with a boundary violation, our chimp brain may respond with intense emotions like anger or fear, making it difficult to assert ourselves calmly and effectively. This can hinder our ability to navigate boundary violations because our emotional reactions may overshadow our rational thinking.

Peters also describes the concept of autopilot, where the chimp brain instinctively controls our thoughts and actions, leading to automatic responses. This is linked to gremlins, or negative thoughts and beliefs from the chimp brain that can hinder our progress and happiness. Peters highlights the importance of identifying and challenging these gremlins to turn them into more helpful autopilot activities to regain control of our lives and avoid self-sabotage.

When our boundaries are crossed, the chimp brain can take over, triggering physical reactions like a faster heart rate, increased alertness and the release of stress hormones like cortisol.

Navigating neurodiversity

Managing the impulsive chimp brain can be more difficult for neurodivergent individuals due to differences in how their brains function. These neurological variations can heighten emotional responses, making it harder to control reactions when boundaries are crossed. Without understanding these reactions, it may be tough to manage emotions like anger, anxiety or frustration, thus complicating boundary-setting. Developing strategies that help with emotional regulation enables neurodivergent people to set boundaries with more confidence and control.

Chapter 6: Trigger Points

A PERSONAL PERSPECTIVE

Looking back, I recognise numerous instances where my instinctive reactions, driven by my chimp brain, took over before I had a chance to process them. These moments usually occurred during periods of high stress, when I was overwhelmed with work and other things happening in my life.

While in the military, I struggled with recurring bouts of depression and anxiety, often breaking down emotionally with outbursts that seemed (to others) like overreactions. At one point, I even came close to being medically discharged because I could not control my emotions.

My ADHD/ASD diagnosis has allowed me to understand the emotional intensity I often felt. It also explained why minor triggers sometimes led to overwhelming emotional responses. Recognising this dynamic has been pivotal in processing my emotional reactions and how they've influenced my behaviour. It has empowered me to manage stress more effectively and recognise how my chimp brain has impacted my decision-making. While I haven't completely eliminated these reactions, I've learned to reduce their frequency and intensity, building greater control and resilience in difficult situations.

A positive aspect of my diagnosis is understanding why I can hyper-focus and be extremely passionate about issues that others might ignore or see as someone else's concern. While this has sometimes been a challenge, my intense passion can lead to positive outcomes when managed well. However, I need to be more mindful of social cues and behaviours, as I sometimes unintentionally overstep other people's boundaries or am too lenient with my own, often to my detriment.

Trauma responses to boundary violations

Over the past century, research on trauma responses to stress has revealed a range of reactions. In the 1920s, physiologist Walter Cannon identified the well-known fight or flight response. Since then, the freeze, fawn, flood and flop responses have been added.

The range of reactions to traumatic events reflects the body's built-in survival mechanisms. These six distinct responses (Figure 6) protect us from perceived danger and are essential for survival during stressful boundary violations.

Chapter 6: Trigger Points

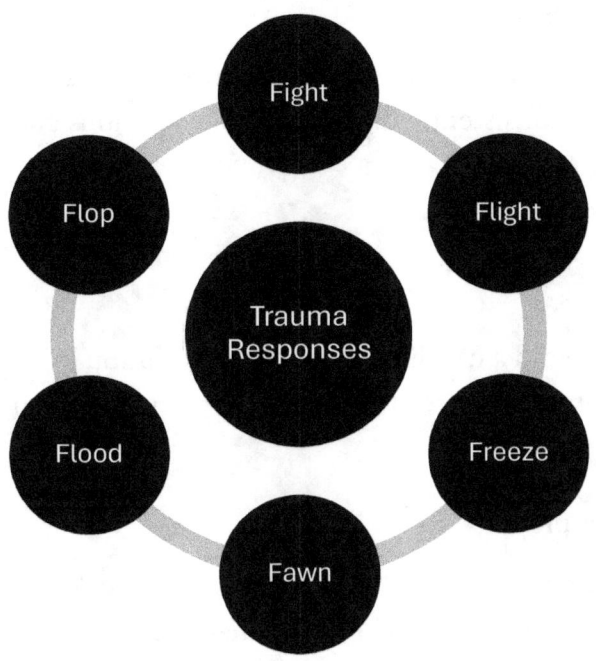

Figure 6: The six Fs of trauma responses

Fight

Instead of assertively confronting a person, you aggressively confront the boundary violation, vigorously defending your rights and needs with forceful communication and aggressive behaviour.

Work example

You confront your supervisor angrily in a meeting because you are frustrated that they often give you extra work at the last minute. You demand recognition and compensation for being assigned tasks without your agreement.

Personal example

You are fed up with how your partner treats you, so you confront them about consistently dismissing your opinions and feelings in your relationship.

Flight

You try to avoid a conflict or boundary violation by withdrawing from the situation or relationship and seeking safety and distance to protect yourself.

Work example

You feel uncomfortable with your supervisor's inappropriate comments and advances. Rather than confronting them, you request a transfer to a different department or resign to avoid further interactions and protect your boundaries.

Personal example

Feeling overwhelmed by your friend's constant demands for emotional support, you start avoiding their calls and messages, choosing to distance yourself to protect your emotional wellbeing.

Freeze

You become immobilised and unable to respond or react to the boundary violation, feeling overwhelmed or paralysed by the situation.

Work example

When your manager adds more tasks without considering your current workload, you feel overwhelmed and unable to speak up. This leaves you feeling stuck and powerless, making it hard to focus even on simple tasks.

Personal example

When your partner criticises you in front of your family, you feel too embarrassed and afraid of more judgment to respond.

Fawn

You seek to appease or please the person violating the boundary, putting their needs and desires over your own to maintain harmony or avoid conflict.

Work example

Even though you feel uncomfortable with your colleague's constant criticism, you continue to seek their approval, changing your work to meet their expectations and avoiding conflict to maintain a good relationship.

Personal example

Your partner's controlling behaviour makes you uncomfortable, but you keep agreeing to their demands, putting their happiness above your own and sacrificing your independence.

Flood

Being flooded with emotions triggers physical symptoms such as dizziness or nausea when your boundaries are crossed, leading to a lack of response.

Work example

You feel dizzy and light-headed when your boss criticises your performance during a team meeting, causing you to lose focus and struggle to respond.

Personal example

You feel suddenly nauseous when your friend pressures you to lend them money despite your financial limits, leaving you feeling unwell and unable to stand up for your boundaries.

Flop

Passively complying with boundary violations, sacrificing personal needs or values to avoid conflict or disappointment.

Work example

You comply with your colleague's request to stay late and work on a project together, even though you had other plans, sacrificing your personal time and needs to avoid disappointing them.

Personal example

Your family members ignore your request for privacy and continue invading your personal space. You passively tolerate their behaviour, feeling powerless to assert your boundaries and maintain your comfort.

Unfortunately, when your emotional brain reacts, it is usually a subconscious reaction to a threat.

> ## NAVIGATING NEURODIVERSITY
>
> *Neurodiverse individuals, especially those with autism and ADHD, may experience fight, flight, freeze or flood mechanisms more intensely and frequently than neurotypicals. Their hypersensitivity to external stimuli, such as noise, lights, stressors or social cues, and how their brains are wired mean they are more prone to sensory and emotional overload.*
>
> *Overwhelming situations or unexpected changes can trigger emotional flooding, where they become unable to think clearly, communicate effectively or manage their behaviour. This heightened state of overwhelm makes recognising and maintaining personal boundaries challenging, which complicates daily interactions. For neurodiverse individuals, understanding these mechanisms and managing sensory inputs is essential for reducing the frequency and intensity of these emotional reactions.*

Situational responses

Irregular responses can be triggered by situations similar to past traumatic experiences or by stressors that overwhelm one's ability to cope. For example, if someone has experienced physical violence in the past, they may react with a fight or flight response to raised voices or aggressive behaviour. Likewise, environments or people that remind them of past trauma can lead to freeze or fawn responses as a way to protect themselves.

Situations that threaten a person's sense of safety, control or autonomy — like feeling trapped in a confined space or being pressured into unwanted activities — also activate trauma responses. These triggers will vary from person to person based on their unique experiences and sensitivities.

 Guiding questions

1. What specific actions do you take when faced with situations that trigger your stress response?
2. What behaviours do you exhibit when you encounter too many stressors?
3. How would you describe your emotions or reactions when confronted with events that threaten your sense of safety, control or autonomy?

Habitual responses

Inappropriate responses are also activated by habits that were formed as learned survival strategies against past experiences. For example, someone who faced emotional abuse in childhood might develop a habit of people-pleasing or avoiding conflict to reduce distress.

Similarly, when someone with an undiagnosed condition has their boundaries challenged, their responses will include fawning,

Chapter 6: Trigger Points

flooding or passive compliance. A person who grew up in an environment where their safety was constantly at risk may react with a fight or flight response to perceived threats, even in safe situations. These unconscious coping mechanisms are triggered by new events that remind them of past trauma.

> **Guiding questions**
>
> 1. What specific actions do you engage in when faced with situations that trigger trauma responses rooted in past events?
>
> 2. What observable behaviours do you notice in yourself when your boundaries are challenged, activating ingrained coping mechanisms developed from past experiences?
>
> 3. How do you typically express yourself or communicate when encountering present-day events that remind you of past trauma, potentially leading to the activation of maladaptive coping strategies?

Window of tolerance to stress

The 'window of tolerance' refers to the optimal emotional state where we can function well and handle everyday stress. The concept was introduced by psychiatrist Dan Siegel and represents the range of emotional and physical arousal that allows a person to cope effectively with stress.[55] When stressors exceed this window, individuals may experience *hyperarousal* symptoms like anxiety or anger or *hypoarousal* symptoms such as numbness or dissociation, as shown in Figure 7.

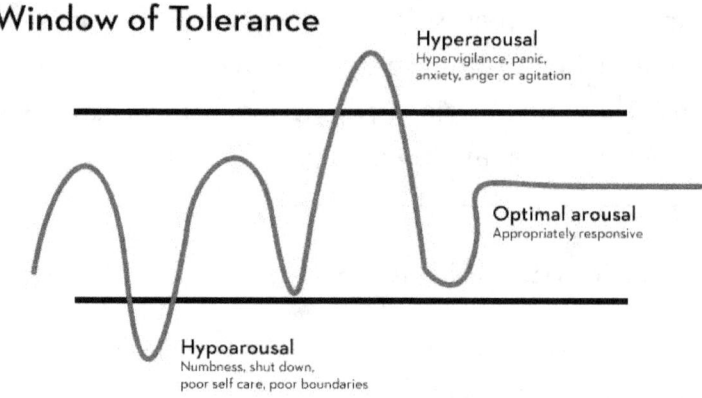

Figure 7: Window of Tolerance (Siegel, 1999)

Can you imagine a situation where you face tight work deadlines, family pressure and ongoing fatigue? If you stay within your window of tolerance, you will manage stress by prioritising tasks and asking for help. However, if your stress exceeds this threshold and you feel your boundaries are violated, it can trigger a trauma response. For instance, depending on the triggers and the relationship involved, you might react by shutting down or lashing out at the person you perceive has crossed your boundaries.

From a low-stress perspective, the window of tolerance is like an athlete's progress in training. As they improve, their window expands, allowing them to try new techniques in a supportive environment. Once these techniques are mastered, they can be applied under pressure in competitions. Ideally, even if athletes perform poorly in practice, they can still do well under stress. Too much stress, however, hinders performance.

Similarly, as individuals grow, their window of tolerance changes. If trauma is not addressed and new coping strategies are not developed, the window will not expand. Like in sports, mastering boundaries takes time. It is essential to start with small boundaries and gradually build up, similar to training for a competition. This approach helps people develop the resilience needed to handle life's challenges.

> **Guiding questions**
>
> 1. When you are within your window of tolerance, what actions do you take to cope effectively with stressors and maintain emotional stability?
>
> 2. How do your behaviours change when stressors exceed the boundaries of your window of tolerance, leading to symptoms of hyper- or hypo-arousal?
>
> 3. What language or verbal cues do you use to express your emotional state when experiencing symptoms of hyper- or hypo-arousal?

Why do we respond the way we do?

Understanding our reactions to boundary violations is a key focus for psychologists and researchers. Factors such as mental health conditions, including autism and ADHD, as well as past traumatic experiences, significantly shape how we respond. These conditions affect our emotional regulation and perception of boundaries, making our reactions more complex.

In his book *The Art of Belonging*, Australian researcher Hugh Mackay examines why we react as we do.[56] He uses a fictional town to illustrate how the strong human need for belonging influences our responses to stress and boundary violations. The desire for social connection means we often choose to protect relationships rather than assert boundaries, fearing rejection or social exclusion.

Our need for belonging can overshadow our instinct to protect ourselves. Trust, intimacy and power dynamics influence different responses to boundary violations in various relationships.

> We often choose to protect relationships rather than assert boundaries.

Close relationships (family and partners) — We often have deeper levels of trust and intimacy in close relationships with family or romantic partners. Boundary violations within relationships trigger strong emotional reactions, such as hurt, betrayal, anger or resentment. For instance, when a partner consistently ignores the other partner's need for personal space and invades their privacy, it can cause feelings of suffocation and emotional distress. This kind of violation seriously affects a person's sense of safety and security in the relationship.

Friends and co-workers — In friendships and workplace relationships, boundaries are more flexible and depend on the context. While there is some trust and familiarity, the power dynamics are not as strong as in close relationships. Boundary violations among friends or coworkers can cause discomfort and strain in interactions, with responses varying based on a person's assertiveness and the seriousness of the violation. For example, a coworker frequently interrupting others during meetings creates tension and disrupts communication. Reactions range from passively accepting the behaviour to assertively confronting it, depending on the person's communication style and how they perceive the potential consequences of speaking up.

Strangers — Interactions with strangers usually involve less emotional investment and intimacy. Boundary violations, such as invading personal space or inappropriate comments, cause discomfort or unease. How people respond may depend on their assertiveness and how threatening they perceive the situation. For instance, if a stranger makes unwanted advances in public, the individual might feel increased stress and discomfort, which could trigger a fight, flight or freeze response based on their window of tolerance to stress.

Figures of perceived authority — Interactions with authority figures, like police officers, emergency responders or doctors, bring extra layers of power dynamics and expectations. People often find these encounters stressful because of the authority these figures hold and the possible consequences of not complying. Boundary violations in these situations prompt responses influenced by fear, respect for authority and past experiences with law enforcement. Overall, how someone reacts to boundary violations depends on their relationship dynamics, assertiveness and the context of the situation.

NAVIGATING NEURODIVERSITY

Navigating boundary violations by neurodivergent individuals, such as frequent interruptions, inappropriate comments or being overly direct, requires clear communication, patience and understanding of their specific needs.

Many neurodivergent individuals, particularly those with ADHD or autism, may struggle to pick up on social cues that indicate when it's appropriate to speak or modify their tone. We can manage this by establishing and reinforcing boundaries through gentle reminders, clear expectations and visual or written cues that guide conversation turn-taking.

Explaining why certain behaviours, such as directness or interrupting, are disruptive helps neurodivergent individuals understand social norms while maintaining their authenticity. Providing structured communication frameworks and offering regular, non-confrontational feedback helps to address boundary violations without creating unnecessary tension or feelings of shame. It is possible to foster a more supportive and inclusive environment by approaching these situations with empathy and understanding.

> **Guiding questions**
>
> 1. What specific actions do you take in response to a boundary being crossed?
> 2. What thoughts or internal dialogue do you observe when you sense your boundaries are being violated?
> 3. How do you notice your behaviours changing when you perceive a boundary violation, compared to when you are in a state of emotional balance?

Suggested responses to boundary violations

Navigating boundary violations in the workplace is essential for maintaining a healthy and productive environment. It is important to respond as diplomatically as possible when these situations arise. Setting clear boundaries and effectively communicating them can prevent future violations. When boundaries are crossed, address the issue promptly and professionally. Suggested responses include calmly expressing your discomfort, firmly but respectfully stating your boundaries and seeking support from a trusted colleague, HR or management if needed.

> **Expressing your feelings when someone crosses your boundaries can be difficult.**

Expressing your feelings when someone crosses your boundaries can be difficult. It is important to remember that some people may not even realise they have done so. While some boundary violations are obvious (see Chapter Three), the person involved might be unaware if you have not previously communicated your boundaries. The following table provides suggested responses for different work situations based on your comfort level with the person crossing the boundary.

- Three stars indicate a high comfort level, allowing for a firm and assertive response.
- Two stars suggest a milder yet effective approach.
- One star indicates situations where your emotional responses might take over, so a softer, less confrontational method is recommended to help you state your boundaries diplomatically.

Each approach has its merits and drawbacks. Whichever you choose, the aim is for the violation to stop.

Chapter 6: Trigger Points

Table 2: Suggested responses to boundary violations

Firm and direct (***)	1. 'I am feeling very uncomfortable with your behaviour. I would like you to respect my boundaries.' Avoid using this response unless you feel extremely threatened and previous assertions have been ignored.
	2. 'I need you to respect my boundaries and give me space.' This response emphasises the need for immediate compliance.
	3. 'I'm not comfortable with this. Please respect my boundaries and stop.'
	4. States your boundaries clearly and directly.
	5. 'I appreciate your concern, but I need you to respect my boundaries. Please refrain from [specific behaviour].' Communicate your discomfort and the need for respect.
	6. 'I understand you may not realise that what you're doing/saying crosses a boundary for me. I need you to stop immediately.' This politely informs the person, clarifies the boundary and requests immediate change without aggression.
	7. 'I must be clear that what you're asking goes against my boundaries. I cannot agree to this.' This firmly communicates that the request is unacceptable, setting a clear, non-negotiable boundary.

Gently asserting yourself (**)	1. 'I feel uncomfortable when you do/say [specific behaviour], and I need you to stop.' This communicates discomfort and directly requests a change in behaviour.
	2. 'Can we talk about this later? I'm feeling overwhelmed right now and need some time alone.' This sets a clear need for space without negating the conversation.
	3. 'Can we talk about this later when I'm feeling more comfortable? I need some space right now.' This gently expresses the need for time alone and promises to address it later.
	4. 'I understand you're trying to help, but I need to handle this on my own. Please respect my space and refrain from [specific behaviour].' This respectfully asks for space while acknowledging the other person's intentions.
	5. 'I'm feeling really overwhelmed right now, and I need some space. Can we please talk about this later when I'm feeling calmer?' This clarifies your emotional state and ensures a future conversation when you are ready.
	6. 'Can we find a different solution that respects my boundaries? I'm not comfortable with this request.' This directly expresses your discomfort and invites a respectful alternative.

Chapter 6: Trigger Points

Passively protecting your boundary (*) Note: this strategy is the least ideal as you are not addressing the issue. Others could misunderstand what you are feeling or expressing.	1. Deflect the behaviour with humour: 'Well, that's one way to make things interesting!' (said with a light chuckle). This response acknowledges the behaviour without escalating it or confronting the violator directly. 2. Subtly disengage from the situation: 'I just remembered I need to grab something, excuse me for a moment.' This allows you to step away from the situation without confronting the person directly. 3. Withdraw from the situation by changing the subject. 'That reminds me, have you heard about [different topic]? It's been quite interesting lately.' This gently redirects the conversation to a more comfortable topic, avoiding the confrontation.

Jefferson Fisher shares practical strategies to stay firm without escalating conflict if you struggle with setting boundaries or responding to dismissive remarks like 'Can't you take a joke?' or 'It's just woke nonsense'. His Instagram @jefferson_fisher includes a great post on maintaining integrity, offering three comebacks that reflect the speaker's words back to them:

'How do you feel when you say that?'
'I'm surprised you said that out loud.'
'Did you mean for that to sound hurtful/rude/ or offensive?'

It is important to note that past traumas or negative experiences related to boundary violations can intensify your emotional responses, leading to stronger reactions. Practising responses will increase your calm in these situations. Ultimately, any perceived threat to autonomy, safety or emotional comfort will activate the emotional brain's defensive mechanisms to protect your wellbeing.

Setting Strong Boundaries

Healthy boundaries are not walls. They are the gates and fences that help you enjoy the beauty of your own garden.
— LYDIA HALL[57]

Establishing and enforcing boundaries empowers you to protect your time, energy and values while fostering respect for yourself and others. Recognising your patterns of behaviour is a key first step in this process.

Recognising your patterns

While researching this book, I came across Rebecca Ray's work on *Setting Boundaries*, which focuses on identifying unhealthy behaviour patterns that weaken our inner strength.[58] Ray points out that a lack of self-worth makes setting boundaries difficult. I know, as it's something I struggled with in the past. She references Eric Berne and his student Frank Ernst's Transactional Analysis theory to explain self-worth issues. This theory examines how people interact using three ego states: Parent, Adult and Child (PAC). It is summarised in Figure 8.

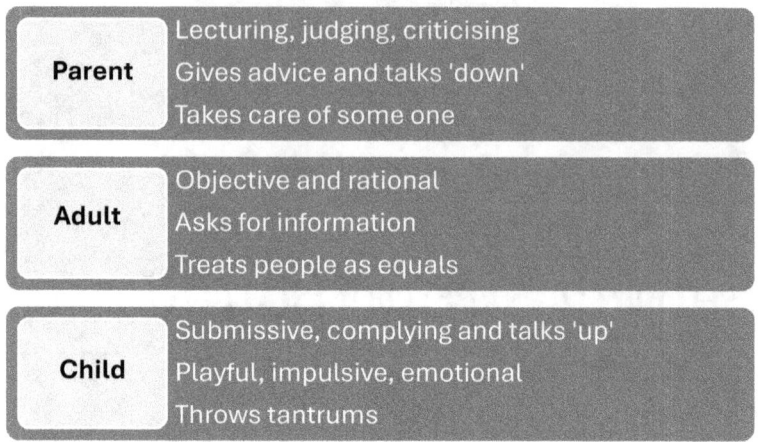

Figure 8: Transactional Analysis — PAC Model (Berne - 1959)

The PAC model explains how people communicate through different ego states, affecting relationship dynamics. The parent state reflects learned behaviours and values from authority figures, the adult state focuses on logical thinking, and the child state represents emotions and instincts. These interactions influence how we behave and connect with others.

For example, in a toxic workplace, a manager (parent) might micromanage an employee (child), disregarding their autonomy and creating an oppressive environment. If, however, an employee (child) consistently misses deadlines, the manager (parent) might step in with discipline to enforce boundaries and ensure accountability.

Chapter 7: Setting Strong Boundaries

A healthier approach for a manager in the (adult) role would involve open communication and collaboration with employees (adult). Instead of micromanaging, the manager could trust the team's abilities and set clear expectations. For example, holding regular meetings to discuss progress and offer support would promote a respectful, trusting environment. This empowers employees to take ownership of their work while maintaining accountability. This approach fosters a positive dynamic where boundaries are respected and employees feel valued and empowered.

Frank Ernst expanded on the PAC model with the OK matrix (Figure 9), which outlines various positions about self-worth and the worthiness of others.[59]

The Boundary Blueprint

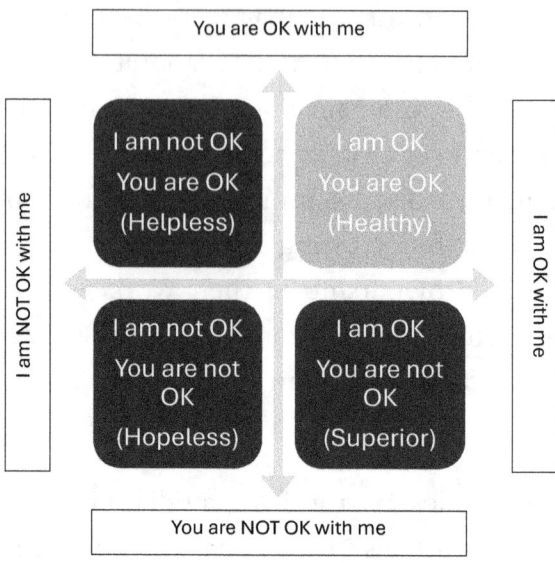

Figure 9: Frank Ernst - OK matrix (1971)

He identified four quadrants in which people communicate. When setting and maintaining boundaries, individuals function within one of these four quadrants.

Helpless — Individuals in this quadrant see themselves as inferior to others, often feeling unworthy or inadequate. This mindset leads to low self-esteem and a weak sense of personal value, which can result in poor boundaries. A person who feels helpless and inferior might mentally tell themselves, *'I'm not as good as others'* or *'I can't do this like they can.'*

Hopeless — People in this quadrant often feel trapped and defeated, believing they lack control over their circumstances. They may view themselves as victims, struggling with blurred boundaries and feeling powerless to improve their situation. This mindset can lead them to think, *'I have no control, and nothing I* *do will make a difference.'* Such thinking reflects a sense of being stuck and unable to make changes.

Superior — People in this quadrant believe they are superior to others, often displaying arrogance or condescension. They see themselves as more important, making it hard for them to connect with others. These individuals tend to have rigid boundaries. They usually have the *'It's my way or the highway'* mentality.

Healthy — The healthy quadrant reflects a balanced view of self and others. People here value themselves and respect others' rights and worth. This mindset supports good relationships, communication and personal growth. They have flexible boundaries that adapt to the situation and relationship.

Knowing which quadrant you usually operate in helps you balance assertiveness and empathy, leading to better relationships. The way you interact with others and view your self-worth affects how you set and maintain boundaries with different people.

Unhealthy boundaries

Identifying unhealthy boundaries is essential for personal growth, empowerment and healthy relationships. These patterns affect wellbeing and interactions. Identifying them enables us to address underlying issues, set better limits and build self-awareness and resilience. We can assert our needs and create boundaries that support emotional wellbeing and genuine connections.

Psychological models like the Parent-Adult-Child framework and the OK matrix provide insight into our interactions. Additional tools, such as the Karpman Drama Triangle (Figure 10), highlight unhealthy relationship patterns and nudge us to break free from roles that limit us.

Karpman Drama Triangle

The Karpman Drama Triangle, created by Stephen B. Karpman (Figure 10), explains harmful relationship dynamics, especially around setting boundaries.[60] The model identifies three roles people take on (often unconsciously) during conflicts: persecutor, victim and rescuer.

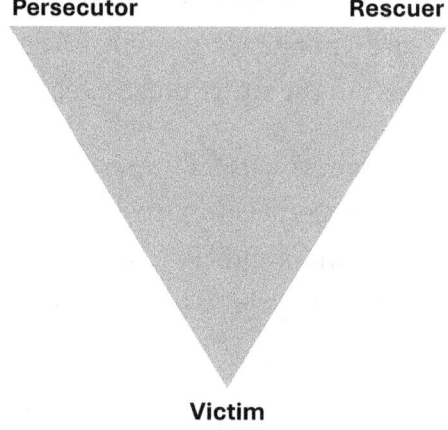

Figure 10: Karpman Drama Triangle (1968)

We often shift between these roles, driven by underlying motives, instead of fixing the main issue. People feel justified in their roles but miss the real problems. This pattern affects how we set and keep boundaries, as we may stay trapped in victim, persecutor or rescuer roles without resolving the actual conflict.

The Persecutor takes a controlling and blaming approach, insisting that others are always at fault. They are often critical, angry and rigid, aiming to dominate others. When confronted, they become defensive or switch to a victim role, leading to a cycle of blame and conflict. Many of us have encountered a persecutor.

For example, in a group project, Emily insisted that only her ideas matter. She dismissed her teammates' suggestions and created a hostile environment. When called on her behaviour, she became defensive and blamed others for not meeting her standards, which caused further conflict and frustration within the team.

The Rescuer often plays the hero, trying to solve other's problems. However, their help can create dependency and stop the person from learning from their experiences. Rescuers may feel guilty if they do not intervene and frustrated when their efforts do not lead to change. They focus on other people's needs to avoid facing their issues, thinking they are genuinely helping, while, in truth, they are simply adding to the drama.

For example, James always stepped in to solve his friends' problems, even when they had not asked for help. By doing this, he reinforced their dependence on him, preventing them from solving issues on their own. His behaviour made James feel needed and important, but it also helped him avoid his own problems.

The Victim feels or acts helpless, seeking sympathy and avoiding responsibility. They see themselves as powerless and look to others as persecutors or rescuers, continuing the cycle of negativity without addressing their own issues.

For example, Cindy constantly complained about her heavy workload and stress but refused to set boundaries with her boss or colleagues. She kept taking on more tasks and worked late, feeling overwhelmed. Instead of addressing the issue, Cindy sought sympathy from friends and family, portraying herself as a victim of circumstances beyond her control.

In any relationship, we can take on the roles of persecutor, victim or rescuer, depending on the situation and the power dynamics at play.

Types of unhealthy boundaries

Boundaries differ from relationship to relationship. Unhealthy boundaries often appear fixed, blurred or non-existent, as shown in Figure 11. These roles can shift based on the situation and the relationship between the people involved, leading to negative feelings and unresolved issues. Understanding these boundary types is necessary because they can worsen conflicts and encourage unhealthy relationship patterns.

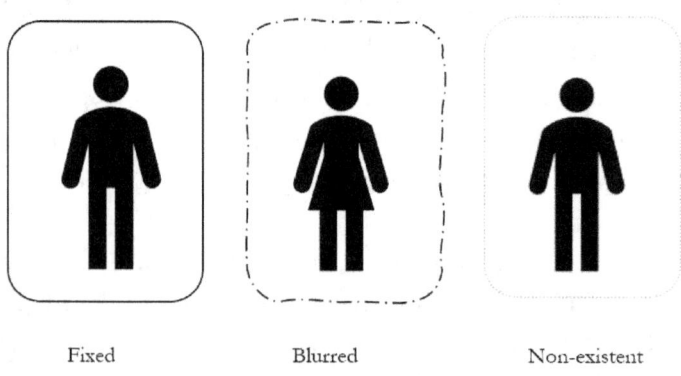

Figure 11: Representation of fixed, blurred and non-existent boundaries

Fixed — Individuals with fixed boundaries have strict, inflexible limits that are hard to change. They resist attempts to adjust

Chapter 7: Setting Strong Boundaries

or negotiate, making it difficult to form close relationships or adapt to new situations. This rigidity leads too soon to isolation and a lack of emotional closeness. Fixed boundaries are like a brick fence — immovable and creating self-esteem issues if not addressed, similar to having a fixed mindset that blocks others' ideas and emotions.

Using the Karpman Drama Triangle examples, Cindy modelled a fixed boundary by refusing to assert herself at work. She saw herself as helpless, maintaining her victim role without confronting her boss or exploring solutions. This prevented her from finding healthier ways to cope or seek support.

Blurred — Blurred boundaries occur when individuals struggle to define their limits, making it hard to separate their needs from others. People with blurred boundaries often have trouble asserting themselves. They may feel overwhelmed or lose their sense of identity as their personal boundaries merge with others.

An example is James, whose blurred boundary showed in his habit of intervening in his friends' lives without their request. He believed he was helping, but his actions blurred the line between offering support and imposing his will. By playing the hero, James fostered dependency and kept his relationships in a cycle of co-dependency.

Non-existent — Non-existent boundaries occur when individuals lack limits, leaving them open to exploitation, manipulation and emotional harm. People with no boundaries often put others' needs ahead of their own, leading to feelings of powerlessness, resentment and difficulty maintaining healthy relationships.

This can manifest as people-pleasing behaviour, where personal wellbeing is sacrificed to avoid conflict.

For example, Emily's teammates exhibited non-existent boundaries by not addressing her behaviour, allowing her to dominate group discussions with her rigid approach. Emily is a persecutor and does not fit neatly into the fixed, blurred or non-existent boundary model. However, because she imposed her ideas without considering others' perspectives and constantly talked over people, she created a toxic environment where the teammates allowed their boundaries to be violated.

Understanding relationship dynamics and boundaries is important, as we unconsciously fall into familiar behaviour patterns that compromise boundaries. This can result in unhealthy dynamics where individuals overstep others' limits or fail to maintain their own. These patterns often manifest in the roles of victim, rescuer or persecutor, which are commonly seen in conflicts.

Impact of unhealthy boundaries

> Understanding relationship dynamics and boundaries is important.

Unhealthy boundaries, combined with low self-worth, can negatively impact mental health, leading to frustration and feelings of powerlessness. This cycle creates anxiety, depression and low self-esteem, causing stress and isolation. To break free, it is important to recognise these patterns, seek support and practice self-care.

Chapter 7: Setting Strong Boundaries

Building self-compassion and assertiveness helps create healthier boundaries and fosters resilience.

I have learned to embrace the qualities of self-awareness, self-compassion and self-acceptance, strengthening my boundaries and confidently expressing my needs. Through personal growth, I moved from being a victim of circumstance to empowerment, prioritising my wellbeing with clear boundaries. As I share my experiences in the following chapters, I invite you to reflect on your boundaries and where adjustments may be needed for a healthier, more fulfilling life.

Empowerment through learning

It is useful to explore models that promote healthier relationships to move away from negative interactions and conflict-driven roles. The Empowerment Dynamic (TED)[61] model offers a positive alternative to the patterns found in the Karpman Drama Triangle (see Figure 12).

The Boundary Blueprint

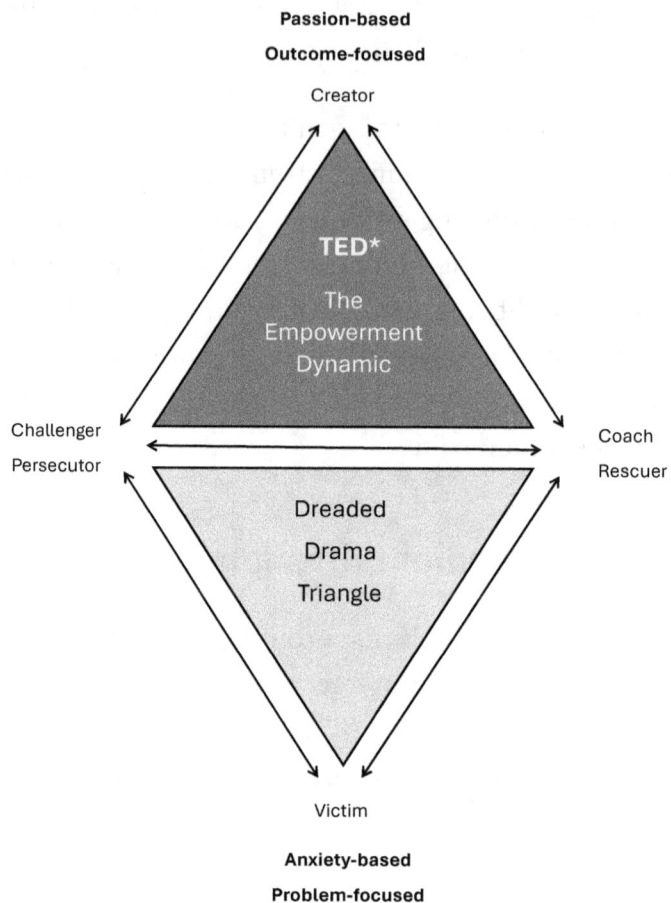

Figure 12: The Empowerment Dynamic* (PowerofTED.com)

Medical doctor and coach David Emerald introduced The Empowerment Dynamic (TED) model, as a positive shift in relationship dynamics. Building on the Karpman drama triangle, TED replaces the negative roles of Victim, Persecutor and Rescuer with the empowering roles of Creator, Challenger and Coach. This approach encourages individuals to focus on goals and outcomes, reinforcing positive boundaries and promoting personal growth and empowerment.

In the TED model, the Victim role transforms into the Creator. Instead of feeling powerless and overwhelmed by problems, the Creator focuses on goals and long-term visions. They take proactive steps toward achieving outcomes and view obstacles as challenges that clarify goals, promoting a more empowered and positive approach to life's difficulties.

The transition from Persecutor to Challenger shifts from blaming and criticising others to encouraging growth and learning. The Challenger helps others step out of their comfort zones and take small steps towards their goals, promoting respect and personal growth.

The shift from Rescuer to Coach involves empowering others to solve their own problems instead of trying to save them. A Coach sees people as capable and supports them by asking guiding questions rather than providing solutions, reinforcing independence and healthy boundaries.

This approach helps individuals redefine their roles and create healthier boundaries. As a coach, I sometimes use this model to guide clients toward taking ownership of their boundaries, empowering them to move beyond victim, perpetrator or rescuer roles. I challenge their behaviour and coach them through different scenarios, helping them become creators of their future.

Applying TED to positive boundaries

Self-leadership and awareness — TED promotes self-leadership by recognising your roles and behaviours. Understanding whether you are acting as a victim, rescuer or persecutor allows you to intentionally shift towards becoming a creator, challenger or coach.

Goal-oriented focus — TED helps individuals set boundaries that support their long-term goals by focusing on outcomes. This clarity prevents them from slipping into reactive and disempowering behaviours.

Empowerment and responsibility — Embracing the creator role empowers individuals to take responsibility for their actions and decisions and set boundaries that promote growth and wellbeing.

Encouragement and support — The challenger and coach roles support others without crossing boundaries. Challengers encourage growth, while coaches offer guidance, each respecting the others' autonomy and abilities.

Whether you act as a victim, rescuer or persecutor, TED shifts you to more empowering roles. You can tap into the creator's creativity, benefit from the challenger's feedback and grow with the coach's support. This change improves relationships and enables you to set positive boundaries for a more fulfilling, passion-driven life.

Boundary diagnostic

Use the following table and reflect on your own experiences, can you identify situations where your boundaries have been challenged or disregarded?

Chapter 7: Setting Strong Boundaries

Table 3: How healthy are your boundaries

Diagnostic area	Healthy boundaries	Unhealthy boundaries
Personal relationships and people pleasing behaviour. How do you respond to people when you are asked to do something you do not want to do?	You recognise the importance of advocating for your needs and assertively communicating boundaries in relationships, fostering mutual respect and understanding.	You consistently prioritise others' needs over your own, avoiding confrontation and sacrificing your wellbeing to maintain harmony, leading to feelings of resentment and dissatisfaction.
Over-extending yourself and self-care activities. How do you prioritise yourself when it comes to self-care and balancing priorities?	You prioritise self-care and balance, setting limits on commitments and learning to say no when necessary to preserve your wellbeing.	You habitually overextend yourself to meet the demands of others, neglecting your own needs and leading to burnout and exhaustion.
Identifying boundary violations. Can you identify instances where you have felt uncomfortable with others when they cross your boundaries?	You identify the behaviour that made you uncomfortable and assertively communicate your boundaries to prevent similar situations in the future.	You struggle to recognise and assert your boundaries, allowing others to repeatedly disrespect or overstep them, leading to frustration and resentment.
Self-reflection of your values and your boundaries. Do you have healthy boundaries or could you improve?	You reflect on past experiences and learn from them, asserting your boundaries assertively and seeking mutually respectful relationships.	You have a pattern of tolerating behaviour that disregards your needs or values, failing to assert boundaries and compromising your wellbeing to maintain relationships.

Diagnostic area	Healthy boundaries	Unhealthy boundaries
Asserting boundaries. Do you say yes when you really want to say no? What prevented you from asserting your boundaries in those moments?	You recognise the importance of honouring your own needs and values, working to overcome fear or guilt and assertively communicating your boundaries.	You struggle with asserting yourself, often giving in to pressure or fear of conflict and sacrificing your wellbeing to avoid disappointing others.
Recall a time when you felt drained or overwhelmed by someone else's demands or expectations. How did you navigate that situation? What boundaries could you have set to protect your wellbeing?	You reflect on the situation and identify the boundaries you could have set to protect your wellbeing, committing to assert them in similar situations in the future.	You feel overwhelmed and drained by others' demands but fail to recognise or assert your boundaries, leading to continued stress and depletion.
Reflect on your inner dialogue when faced with a challenging interaction. Do you find yourself minimising your feelings or justifying others' behaviour at the expense of your boundaries?	You acknowledge and validate your feelings, recognising the importance of prioritising your boundaries and wellbeing in interactions.	You tend to minimise or ignore your feelings, justifying others' behaviour and neglecting your boundaries, leading to a pattern of self-sacrifice and dissatisfaction.

Chapter 7: Setting Strong Boundaries

Diagnostic area	Healthy boundaries	Unhealthy boundaries
Consider the dynamics within your social circle or family. Are there recurring patterns of behaviour or expectations that leave you feeling restricted or unheard? How do you navigate these dynamics while honouring your boundaries?	You recognise and address recurring patterns that disregard your boundaries, assertively communicating your needs and values to maintain healthy relationships.	You feel restricted or unheard in your social circle or family dynamics but struggle to assert your boundaries or communicate your needs, leading to feelings of resentment and alienation.
Think about your physical and emotional responses when your boundaries are tested. How do you feel? What do these reactions reveal about your boundaries?	You recognise your physical and emotional responses as signals that your boundaries are being tested, prompting you to assert them assertively and protect your wellbeing.	You experience tension, anxiety or resentment in boundary-testing situations but fail to recognise or address these reactions, allowing others to continue disregarding your boundaries.
Reflect on your past experiences with setting boundaries. Where have you made progress? Do you notice recurring challenges? What lessons can you draw from these experiences to strengthen your boundary-setting skills?	You acknowledge areas of progress in setting boundaries, learning from past challenges to strengthen your boundary-setting skills and promote healthier relationships.	You encounter recurring challenges in setting boundaries, struggling to assert yourself and experiencing repeated boundary violations, indicating a need for further development in boundary-setting skills.

The Boundary Blueprint

Diagnostic area	Healthy boundaries	Unhealthy boundaries
Consider the role of guilt or fear in your decision-making process when asserting boundaries. How do these emotions influence your ability to consider your own needs and values first?	You recognise and address feelings of guilt or fear that hinder your ability to assert boundaries, working to prioritise your own needs and values in decision-making.	You often prioritise others' needs over your own due to feelings of guilt or fear, neglecting your boundaries and compromising your wellbeing in the process.
Imagine your ideal scenario for setting and maintaining boundaries in your life. What would that look like? What steps can you take to align your actions with your boundaries?	You envision clear and assertive communication of your boundaries, fostering mutual respect and understanding in your relationships. You take proactive steps to assert and maintain boundaries aligned with your needs and values.	You aspire to set and maintain boundaries effectively in your life but struggle to envision or implement clear boundaries, leading to your boundaries being violated.

Exploring these questions and reflecting on your past experiences offers a clearer understanding of where your boundaries stand in different areas of your life. This self-awareness is the first step to defining and respecting your boundaries. In the following chapters, you will learn practical strategies to enforce healthier boundaries, helping you build more fulfilling and balanced relationships.

Challenging Gender Bias

Each time a woman stands up for herself, without knowing it, she stands up for all women.

— MAYA ANGELOU [62]

Boundary violations in the workplace often relate to gender bias, creating challenges for women trying to advance in their careers. Women frequently experience being interrupted in meetings, having their ideas taken or facing microaggressions — all are rooted in deep-seated gender biases.

Microaggressions are subtle comments or actions that reinforce gender bias, often unintentionally. They include dismissive remarks, questioning competence or ignoring women's ideas until repeated by men. Though seemingly minor, these violations damage trust and confidence while reinforcing negative stereotypes and leading to ongoing inequality. Addressing these is crucial for combating gender bias and creating an environment where everyone thrives.

This chapter explores the specific challenges women face in non-traditional roles and STEM careers as they work to assert their boundaries, navigate workplace dynamics and overcome gender stereotypes. By understanding and addressing these issues, women can empower themselves to create environments that support their growth, wellbeing and professional success.

Historical gender barriers

The movie *Hidden Figures* is based on the true story of three African-American women mathematicians who played key roles in the NASA space program in the early 1960s. In one powerful scene, Katherine G. Johnson (Taraji P. Henson) explains that it takes her forty minutes to use the restroom because she must walk half a mile to use a segregated women's facility. In a stand against gender and racial barriers, her manager, Al Harrison (Kevin Costner), removes the sign.[63]

Closer to home, Australia, like many other nations, has not been exempt from overlooking basic facilities for women, even in its federal parliament. Despite electing female representatives in 1943, it was not until 1974 that the Australian Federal Parliament installed its first designated female toilets. Until then, female parliamentarians had to rely on facilities intended for staff and visitors, underscoring the lack of attention given to women's needs in positions of power at the time.[64]

Chapter 8: Challenging Gender Bias

Missing mentors

Women often struggle to access training and mentorship in STEM fields. Research shows that this affects the low representation of women, with fewer researchers willing to mentor female candidates and their achievements frequently going unrecognised. A 2021 study by Doaa Khalil, a University of Southern Maine researcher, revealed that lack of support alongside workplace culture issues (like boundary violations) can lead some women to leave or change careers.[65]

Khalil noted that women often face difficulties gaining recognition and respect in STEM, leading to insecurity and self-doubt. Her thesis highlighted that many women she interviewed were advised to pursue non-STEM degrees or change careers because they were perceived as unable to succeed in their chosen fields. Despite these challenges, many women in STEM work hard to prove themselves, often facing more pressure and stress than their male peers.

The Boundary Blueprint

The double-bind

Australian author and leadership expert Anneli Blundell explores the challenges women face in her book, *The Gender Penalty*.[66] She explains that traditional leadership stereotypes favour men, allowing them to navigate the professional world easily — as if playing a game with rules designed to benefit them. In contrast, when women try to follow the same rules and challenge societal expectations, they often face penalties and disapproval. This limited view of leadership stifles creativity and diversity, reducing the potential for everyone involved.

Authentic leadership should embrace different strategies and empower everyone to contribute their strengths, reshaping the workplace to be more inclusive and fair.

However, it is important to recognise that this issue is not just about men versus women. There is tension between individual fairness and organisational competition, especially since male CEOs lead many companies. The focus on competition can lead organisations to prioritise personal interests over fairness. This is seen in the 'professionalisation' of human resources (HR), which often serves organisational needs, even though many HR representatives are women. Furthermore, the association of competition with male traits and liberalism with feminism may reinforce gender biases, with some men viewing liberal approaches as less competitive, perpetuating disparities in leadership perceptions.

> This issue is not just about men versus women.

Global management consultants McKinsey & Company found that profits increase by 2.4% for every 10% rise in gender diversity among senior leadership teams.[67] Further, research from First Round Capital showed that companies with at least one female founder had investment returns that were 63% higher than all-male teams.[68] These findings highlight the financial advantages of diverse perspectives in decision-making and emphasise the importance of women's contributions.

However, many talented women face a double bind in today's workplace. If they adopt traditionally masculine traits, they may be seen as too aggressive, but if they embrace feminine characteristics, they risk being overlooked for leadership roles. This issue, known as the gender penalty, prevents women from reaching their full potential in the workplace, affecting not just those in STEM but all women in male-dominated environments.

> Many talented women face a double bind in today's workplace.

Research from the University of Toronto highlights the double bind phenomenon, where assertive women are seen as competent but less likeable, which can harm their career growth.[69] This double standard penalises women whether they conform to or challenge traditional gender roles, showing the systemic barriers they face.

Further research shows that everyday interactions in male-dominated workplaces affect how women are treated.[70,71] Subtle biases mean women in STEM often report feeling less engaged and more mentally drained after interacting with some male colleagues.

These negative experiences contribute to a high turnover, known as the 'leaky pipeline', as many women leave the industry to find workplaces where they feel valued.[72] It highlights the urgent need for cultural change in STEM fields.

Common stereotypes of women in STEM

In the male-dominated world of STEM, women face many stereotypes that affect how others view their abilities and goals, creating biases that hinder their progress. These stereotypes are deeply ingrained in society and reinforced through various means, negatively impacting women's experiences in STEM and limiting their access to opportunities.

From assumptions about technical incompetence to beliefs about emotional weakness, women encounter prejudiced attitudes that diminish their contributions and potential. Understanding and challenging these stereotypes is crucial to creating an inclusive and equitable environment where women can set and maintain boundaries.

Consider these common stereotypes about women in non-traditional roles or STEM fields.

Not technically proficient

Women in STEM are often misidentified as less skilled or proficient than their male colleagues, reinforcing the idea that confidence sometimes overshadows competence. This bias can leave women underestimated or overlooked for technical roles, even when they are fully qualified. For example, a female technician might be seen as less capable of solving technical issues simply because of her gender.

I experienced this bias firsthand as an avionics technician, where my suggestions for troubleshooting a particular problem on an aircraft were ignored until a male colleague shared the same idea. At that point, it was accepted as a valid solution.

Lack leadership abilities

There is a notion that women lack the skills or suitability for leadership roles in STEM fields. This bias often leads to women being overlooked for promotions or leadership positions, even when they have the necessary experience. For example, a woman with extensive experience and proven leadership skills might be passed over for a managerial role in favour of a less experienced male candidate, reinforcing the belief that women are less effective leaders.

Anneli Blundell points out that men often only need to show the potential for leadership, while women typically must have considerable experience to be considered suitable for such roles.[73] This contradiction creates a catch-22 situation: how can women gain the required expertise if they are not given the opportunity to showcase their abilities and potentially outperform their male counterparts?

Emotional or overly sensitive

Women are often seen as more emotional or sensitive than men, which can be viewed as a disadvantage in STEM fields that value logic and objectivity. Women may face criticism for showing emotions at work. For example, if a female scientist feels disappointed or frustrated after receiving feedback on her research project, she might be labelled overly emotional, while similar reactions from male colleagues may not receive the same negative perception.

Early biases discourage STEM

Children's understanding of gender is shaped and reinforced early by family dynamics, cultural influences, media representations, school settings and societal norms. Recent research shows that young girls often absorb the stereotype that STEM is male-dominated, which lowers their confidence and interest in pursuing STEM careers.[74] This bias starts around ages four to five when children begin to form their gender identities and may avoid behaviours associated with the opposite sex to fit societal expectations. If these biases are not addressed, they can continue to influence career choices and reinforce the idea that STEM is primarily for males.

> Even well-intentioned friends and family inadvertently discourage girls from considering STEM careers.

This research highlights a critical barrier to gender equality in these careers. The fact that these biases take root in the preschool years reveals how deeply societal expectations influence self-perception and interests in young girls. If left unchallenged, this early internalisation can shape their educational and career choices, perpetuating the stereotype that STEM is better suited for males. As a result, girls are often subtly discouraged from pursuing interests in maths and science, which perpetuates the stereotype that women are less capable in these fields. This bias creates obstacles in education, career paths and workplace dynamics, hindering women's advancement and opportunities for success.

CASE STUDY: BREAK STEREOTYPES TO INSPIRE YOUNG MINDS

There's a powerful YouTube video of a classroom where children were asked to draw common professions like police officers, firefighters, doctors and pilots. Sixty-one children portrayed these professionals as male figures and only five as female, reflecting societal stereotypes.

Afterwards, professionals from these fields visited the classroom. To the children's surprise, the visitors were a female police officer, a female firefighter, a female doctor and a female pilot.

The children's initial reaction was confusion and disbelief as they encountered professionals who did not fit their expectations. However, as the women shared their experiences, the mood changed. The children listened closely, asked questions and admired these women for breaking barriers in traditionally male-dominated careers.

By the end of the session, the children's perceptions had shifted. They realised that gender does not determine abilities or career choices. They were left inspired and eager to challenge stereotypes and explore their potential without gender limitations. The video is well worth a watch. https://www.youtube.com/watch?v=qv8VZVP5csA. *Show it to the young people in your life.*

Chapter 8: Challenging Gender Bias

The influence of neurological wiring

This case study highlights the importance of exposing children to diverse role models early in their lives and continually engaging them with the wide range of careers that women follow, to broaden their understanding of gender roles and possibilities. By challenging stereotypes and celebrating diversity, educators and parents can help shape a more inclusive and equitable future for the next generation.

However, Simon Baron-Cohen's work challenges the traditional view that gender influences one's aptitude in science and math. His research, documented in *The Essential Difference*, highlights that it is not gender but rather neurological wiring that predisposes individuals to excel in these fields.[75] According to Baron-Cohen, people with a more 'systemising' brain (often observed in those with autism), have a natural inclination toward understanding systems, patterns and abstract reasoning. This cognitive style, rather than gender, can explain why some individuals are more drawn to and excel in subjects like science and maths. This finding should be widely shared to dispel the stereotype that girls are no good at maths and science.

You can't be what you can't see

Women in STEM are often told that they do not belong in male-dominated environments. This feeling of not fitting in can lead to isolation, imposter syndrome and a lack of confidence. For instance, a female computer programmer may be the only woman on her team, making her feel out of place and reinforcing the idea that she does not belong.

'You can't be what you can't see,' said Marian Wright Edelman, a civil and children's rights activist who believed children are less likely to be inspired if they don't have visible role models. Her wise words highlight the importance of role models in shaping career aspirations.

Edelman's quote was illustrated in the documentary *Miss Representation*, which highlights how mainstream media perpetuates the underrepresentation of women in leadership positions, a trend also seen in STEM fields.[76] The film reveals how media portrayals often limit women's roles and influence, creating barriers to entry for girls aspiring to pursue science, technology, engineering and mathematics. These cultural stereotypes hinder the recognition and promotion of women in STEM, emphasising the need for broader representation and the dismantling of limiting narratives in both media and educational systems. Unfortunately, parents and other women can unintentionally discourage girls from pursuing fields where they are underrepresented.

While mentoring high school students, I realised I had no female role models in my military career. A remark from someone I respected, suggesting that I stick to 'women's work', fuelled my determination to prove them wrong. Consequently, I deliberately entered a trade within the military with minimal female representation, driven by indignation and a desire to challenge this stereotype. Little did I know the significant impact of this decision on my life and career trajectory. Today, I serve as a role model for girls and women who, like me, lacked representation and encouragement in their career pursuits.

Chapter 8: Challenging Gender Bias

> **CASE STUDY: UNINTENTIONAL BARRIERS**
>
> *I arrived at an appointment with my doctor wearing my military uniform. The medical receptionist inquired about my profession within the military, to which I responded that I was an engineer. Her response was disheartening. She said she would never advise her daughter to pursue engineering, citing doubts about her aptitude and concerns about potential mistreatment by male colleagues in the industry. This encounter is a stark reminder that even well-intentioned friends and family inadvertently discourage girls from considering STEM careers.*

Achieving gender parity in male-dominated industries, such as STEM, finance and manufacturing, is a long-term challenge. Societal biases and stereotypes, which begin in childhood, discourage girls from pursuing these careers. The World Economic Forum estimates that, at the current pace, it may take around 135 years to achieve global gender parity.[77] This slow progress mirrors the prolonged struggle for racial equality, highlighting the need for sustained, multifaceted efforts.

Assumptions about career priorities

The remaining stereotype to discuss is that women always prioritise family over their careers, leading to assumptions about their commitment to work. This results in women being overlooked for challenging projects or promotions. For example, a female engineer who declines overtime or travel due to family commitments when her children are young may be seen as less dedicated compared to her male colleagues despite her qualifications and commitment.

While in the military, my engineering officer incorrectly determined that, as a single parent, I could not take on sea duty because he wrongly assumed I had sole custody of my children.

Women in STEM are not passive victims of these stereotypes or boundary violations; many are resilient and determined to challenge and overcome them.

Fostering an inclusive work environment

While government roles offer equal pay regardless of gender, private sector wage gaps persist due to biases in male-dominated industries. These biases limit women's opportunities to reach leadership positions compared with men. Creating an inclusive work environment means addressing biases and ensuring equal opportunities regardless of gender.

Australia's national gender pay gap currently sits at an average of 21.7%, according to the Workplace Gender Equality Agency's 2024 report.[78] These statistics confirm the ongoing gender gap holding women from participating in an inclusive workforce. Women face systemic inequities, especially in private sector roles, where hidden biases affect pay and career advancement. Private industry undervalues women's contributions, unlike government jobs that offer equal pay. This highlights the need for structural

Chapter 8: Challenging Gender Bias

changes to remove barriers, ensure fair pay and create leadership opportunities for women, building a truly inclusive workforce.

Over 62% of Australian companies have a gender pay gap favouring men, showing the systemic nature of wage inequality. This disparity highlights ongoing challenges in getting fair pay and advancement in male-dominated fields for women. Despite some progress, the persistent pay gap and resistance to gender equity reveal a significant obstacle to creating fair workplaces. Addressing these issues is essential because research shows that companies with diverse leadership perform better in innovation and financial results. Breaking down these barriers benefits gender equality and overall workforce potential, driving growth for everyone.

> **Creating an inclusive work environment is a shared responsibility.**

Creating an inclusive work environment is a shared responsibility that requires effort from everyone in the organisation.

Initiatives such as the Science in Australia Gender Equity (SAGE), Athena SWAN accreditation by the Commonwealth Scientific and Industrial Research Organisation (CSIRO) aim to promote gender equality and support women in these fields by creating more inclusive work environments.[79] If you want to know more, the Diversity Council of Australia website https://www.dca.org.au/ offers valuable insights into what it means to be genuinely inclusive.[80]

Whatever their role or background, each person plays a part in fostering a space where all individuals feel valued, respected and empowered to share their unique skills and perspectives. In STEM and other non-traditional fields, women need to support one another, helping to break barriers, amplify voices and create a more inclusive and prosperous environment for all.

Breaking the cycle

While I have seen significant improvements in how women are treated over the past thirty years, progress is needed in creating an inclusive environment where women's talents are fully recognised. Despite the obstacles of societal norms, stereotypes and self-doubt, these challenges also present opportunities for empowerment and growth. Identifying and confronting these barriers means women harnessing their resilience and determination to succeed in male-dominated fields. By actively working to dismantle gender bias and redefine expectations, women can thrive and promote greater inclusivity in the workplace. There are several ways to achieve this.

Communicating with confidence

Break the cycle of being interrupted or talked over by asserting themselves confidently in meetings and discussions. For example, using assertive language such as 'I have something to add' or 'Let me finish my point' can help women command respect and ensure their voices are heard. Depending on your level of confidence, you could use one of the following statements. As you read them,

Chapter 8: Challenging Gender Bias

remember the three levels of response discussed at the end of Chapter Four.

>****'Excuse me, I wasn't finished speaking. I'd appreciate your letting me complete my thoughts before interjecting.'*

>***'I understand your point, and I'll get to it shortly. Let me finish my current thought, and then I'll be glad to hear your input.'*

>**'I'm sorry to interrupt, but I'd like to finish my point before we move on. Could you please give me a moment to do so?'*

Seeking leadership opportunities

If you want to pursue leadership roles but feel held back by gender bias, tackle this challenge directly. Start conversations about your leadership goals, seek out leadership projects, express interest in managerial positions and connect with successful female mentors. Use your annual performance reviews to display your leadership potential and ambitions. The following table offers suggestions for navigating your next performance evaluation.

Direct	'I'd like to discuss opportunities for leadership roles within the team. I believe my skills and experience align well with the responsibilities of such positions, and I'm eager to take on additional challenges and contribute to the team's success. Can we explore potential pathways for me to step into leadership roles and ways to support my development in that direction?'

Collaborative	'I've been reflecting on ways I can further contribute to our team's goals. I'm interested in exploring leadership opportunities and would appreciate your guidance on how I can develop the necessary skills and experience. I value your insights and would like to work together to identify areas where I can grow and take on more responsibility within the team.'
Future-oriented	'Looking ahead, I'm excited about the possibility of expanding my role within the team and taking on leadership responsibilities. I've been actively developing my leadership skills, and I'm committed to contributing to the team's success in a more strategic capacity. I'd like to discuss how we can align my career aspirations with the organisation's goals and identify opportunities for me to grow and advance professionally.'

There are other paths, too. Many people mistakenly believe that pursuing leadership or management roles is the only way to advance in their careers, which can lead to dissatisfaction. This misconception arises from limited awareness of alternative career paths.

In STEM fields, companies now offer a range of career streams, showing that management is not the only option for advancement. For instance, I hold a non-traditional position outside management in my current role as a subject matter expert (SME) in safety engineering. However, companies must establish fair pay structures for non-managerial roles to prevent confusion about compensation and career growth.

This issue is compounded by existing biases against women, who often face discrimination in obtaining leadership roles and encounter fewer higher-paying paths outside of management. As a result, more women occupy lower-paying positions. In contrast, men dominate higher-paying ones, highlighting institutional differences in roles rather than a straightforward pay gap for similar positions.

Advocating for equal treatment

Women can break the misconception of being perceived as overly sensitive by advocating for fair and equal treatment in the workplace. That includes addressing instances of gender bias or discrimination directly with management. You can directly address cases of gender bias and discrimination in the following ways. Again, note the three levels of potential responses.

*****'I've noticed a pattern of behaviour in the workplace that concerns me. There have been instances where I feel unfairly treated or marginalised based on my gender. I'd like to discuss these issues openly and work together to ensure a fair and inclusive environment for all employees.'*

****'I've noticed some situations at work lately that have made me feel uncomfortable, and I think they might be related to gender bias. I want to bring it to your attention in a constructive way, as I believe it's important for us to foster an environment where everyone feels valued and respected.'*

***'I've observed a few instances recently that have left me feeling uneasy, and I wonder if we could discuss them. I think there might be some unintentional bias at play, and I'd like to explore ways we can address it together to ensure a positive and inclusive workplace for everyone.'*

Additional methods for advocating for equal treatment include enlisting support from allies within the organisation, including male colleagues. For instance:

'I believe that addressing issues of gender bias and discrimination requires collective action. I'm reaching out to you as an ally within the organisation to seek your support in advocating for fair and equal treatment for women in the workplace. Together, we can raise awareness, promote inclusivity and drive positive change.'

You may find it challenging to address the issue directly with the individual involved, so you may opt to use formal channels such as management or HR to raise awareness of the concerning behaviour. If you decide to pursue this avenue, be sure to document specific instances of the behaviour and ensure that you have accurately interpreted the situation before taking further action.

'I want to bring to your attention some concerns I've had regarding gender bias and discrimination in the workplace. I believe addressing these issues through formal channels is important to ensure accountability and promote a culture of respect and equality. Can we schedule a meeting to discuss how we can address these concerns effectively?'

Investing in skills development

Women can overcome the stereotype of inferiority in male-dominated professions by investing in continuous learning and skills development. Participating in such programs can bolster confidence in establishing and reinforcing boundaries, leading to greater assertiveness and effectiveness in the workplace.

Here are some examples:

- **Enrol in training programs** — These programs may encompass technical skill enhancement, leadership development or industry-specific knowledge, offering valuable insights and expertise to empower you to thrive in your role.

- **Attend conferences, workshops or seminars** — These events offer opportunities to learn from industry experts, network with peers and gain practical insights into emerging trends and best practices.

- **Build supportive networks** — Overcome feelings of not belonging by creating supportive networks inside and outside the workplace. Join professional groups, attend networking events and find mentors who can offer guidance and advice. Mentors guide you to navigate challenges and opportunities, making it easier to advance in your career.

- **Demonstrate commitment to your career** — Challenge assumptions about your career priorities by showing dedication and commitment to your work. That includes taking on challenging projects, exceeding expectations and seeking growth opportunities. Chapters Ten, Eleven and Twelve explain how to do this without burning out.

Self-awareness and education

Encouraging continuous learning about implicit bias and stereotyping is essential. Workshops, seminars and training programs can help raise awareness and reduce unconscious bias. Many websites and programs offer helpful information and training on this. For best results, seek training that uses real-life examples and role-playing to help participants experience different perspectives rather than just PowerPoint lectures on research. Engage in activities that show how bias appears in the workplace to help people empathise and understand others.

Mentorship

I strongly advocate for mentorship and was grateful to be awarded Mentor of the Year in 2024 for the Australian Space Awards. I believe formal programs can greatly empower individuals to be assertive. I have mentored for sixteen years and participated in various formal mentorship programs across multiple industries. Some have been excellent, while others were less so. The success of these programs often depends on the quality of the facilitators, their understanding of the industry and the people who want to be mentored. As a mentor, it is important to listen to what is not being said and tailor the advice accordingly.

With many mentorship programs emerging, ensure your mentors are skilled and intentional. To get the most benefit, clarify why you seek mentoring and where you need support. Do this before joining a program.

If you are confident in your boundaries, consider volunteering as a mentor. I have mentored many individuals, including young people, refugee engineers, university students, men transitioning from the defence force and mid-career women. Each experience has given me new perspectives, personal growth and a deeper understanding of diverse backgrounds. Mentoring benefits others and enriches your development.

> ## CASE STUDY: A JOURNEY TO LEADERSHIP IN TECHNOLOGY
>
> *In a busy tech firm, Felicity, a talented software engineer, faced challenges as she worked to prove herself in a male-dominated industry. With the guidance of her mentor, Emily, a seasoned leader who had overcome similar obstacles, Felicity learned to face gender bias confidently.*
>
> *When a high-profile software project came up, Felicity took the lead despite doubts from some colleagues. She drew on Emily's lessons and led her team with determination, overcoming technical and stakeholder challenges. The project was completed ahead of schedule and under budget, earning praise for its innovation.*
>
> *Along the way, Felicity faced doubts and boundary violations from colleagues who questioned her abilities. With her mentor's support and her personal resilience, Felicity pushed through. Her hard work was recognised, and she was promoted to a leadership role, showing that women can succeed in male-dominated fields with persistence and strong mentorship.*

Sponsorship

Male sponsorship in male-dominated industries can be transformative for women's career advancement. By advocating for female colleagues, male sponsors can help close the gender gap, giving women access to key projects, promotions and leadership roles. This support allows women to display their skills and build strong networks while creating a more inclusive and diverse workplace that benefits everyone.

I was incredibly fortunate to have a male naval captain see potential in me in 2007 when I was at a crossroads in my career. Even though I was a single parent, his advocacy for me to undertake formal engineering studies helped me get to where I am today. It was not easy, but without his help, I could not do the work I love or help as many people as I do now. Over the past fifteen years, a few other male champions have supported me, and I am deeply grateful. A simple word of advocacy or suggestion from a male sponsor can significantly change a woman's career path.

Building an inclusive culture

An inclusive culture is critical for women to assert their boundaries because it creates a space where diversity is valued and everyone is heard. In such a culture, women feel safer and more supported, making it easier to express their needs without fear of backlash. When a woman stands up for her boundaries, it sets a powerful example for others, encouraging them to do the same. This helps transform the workplace into a more respectful and equitable space.

> The actions of one person can inspire others.

The actions of one person can inspire others, creating a culture where everyone feels valued and empowered. I know that I thrive physically and mentally in supportive work environments that allow me to bring my best energy and enthusiasm to the job.

Chapter 8: Challenging Gender Bias

Organisational power dynamics

This book would not be complete without addressing the power dynamics within organisations. After over thirty years in a male-dominated environment, I have found that some of my toughest conflicts have been with other women. Especially when women who have faced hardships become obstacles to other women's progress. Understanding this is key to creating a more inclusive workplace.

Women's interactions reveal the complexities of boundaries, showing both the potential for support and the risk of conflict. From mother-daughter relationships to professional collegial settings, these interactions highlight the need for women to navigate boundaries with care and understanding.

When women support each other and are mindful of boundaries, they foster a positive environment that promotes mutual growth. Exploring these dynamics helps us understand how boundary crossings — whether well-meaning or power-driven — significantly shape personal and professional relationships.

Women cross each other's boundaries for many reasons, from good intentions, friendships or a desire for power. Yet even when the intent is positive, such as offering help, there is always the potential for misunderstandings or strain. For example, a well-meaning mother might overstep a boundary with her daughter by giving unsolicited advice or interfering in personal decisions, leaving the daughter frustrated or resentful by undermining her independence. This happens across generations at work, too.

In contrast, boundary violations driven by a need for power, especially at work, are more damaging. A female leader might see other women as threats to her authority and undermine them by micromanaging them, ignoring their ideas or taking credit for their work — much as we see some men behave. But there's a bigger impact when women treat women in this way; it's a kind of betrayal of the feeling that women should have each others' backs when the environment is already tough.

> ### A PERSONAL PERSPECTIVE
>
> *In 2007, as a single parent aiming to become a commissioned officer, I faced unexpected challenges from a female officer trying to exert her power. After passing the university entrance exams, my final step was getting approval from the leadership team. I had the support of a staff officer in Melbourne, who believed in my potential, but I faced resistance from a female officer above her. Without my knowledge, emails circulated questioning my suitability due to being a single parent with limited family support. The higher-ranking officer wanted to deny my application, concerned about my ability to balance studies and family life. Thankfully, someone even higher than her stepped in and approved my application. This experience opened my eyes to the challenges women face when they do not support each other.*

Women supporting women

Women have a powerful opportunity to support each other by consciously respecting boundaries and creating spaces for mutual growth. Research highlights that women who uplift one another in professional settings foster greater collaboration and productivity, counteracting harmful competition.[81]

Strategies to support each other include being open to active listening, offering encouragement and creating safe spaces for honest conversations. For instance, rather than overstepping boundaries by giving unsolicited advice, women can ask how they can assist and provide support. In leadership, a commitment to promoting collaboration over competition helps counteract the risk of undermining others. When women hold each other accountable for maintaining healthy professional boundaries and ensure their interactions are based on respect and empathy, they strengthen the network of women in leadership.

Build positive and supportive alliances by surrounding yourself with inspiring women who can offer strength and resources and counter negative behaviours. Seek mentorship from those who have faced similar challenges. Mentors can offer advice and strategies for managing difficult situations, empowering you to handle tough colleagues.

These practices mean women lead by example, encouraging inclusivity and collaboration across workplaces.

Male colleagues supporting women

I don't blame or shame men for not understanding women's unique challenges — I acknowledge that many men are very supportive. Yet many are unaware of the biases women encounter daily. So, how can we work together to overcome these challenges and achieve equity?

Men can play a key role in creating a supportive and inclusive workplace where women feel respected and empowered. By advocating for women, challenging bias and supporting gender equality, men help create a culture of fairness. In turn, this benefits everyone, including them by improving collaboration, innovation and workplace morale while fostering stronger, more effective teams. Here's how men can do this.

Educate themselves — Learn about gender bias, inequality and women's experiences in the workplace. Read books, attend workshops or training sessions and engage in conversations with female colleagues or mentors.

Listen and amplify — Actively listen to and boost women's perspectives and concerns in the workplace. Give credit to women for their ideas and contributions, ensure that women are included in decision-making processes and speak up when witnessing gender bias or discrimination.

Challenge bias and norms — Challenge harmful norms and behaviours by speaking out against inappropriate actions and supporting policies that foster respect and inclusivity. Question stereotypes and assumptions about gender roles and capabilities by addressing sexist language or behaviour, advocating for equal opportunities and promoting diversity and inclusion initiatives within your organisation.

Be an ally — Actively support and advocate for women's advancement and success in the workplace. Mentor female colleagues, sponsor them for career opportunities and use privilege and influence to create positive change.

Lead by example — Promote gender equality and inclusivity in behaviour and decision-making. Appoint diverse teams and actively seek out and promote women for leadership roles. Be accountable for creating an inclusive work culture.

Continuous learning and growth — Commit to constant learning and development in understanding gender dynamics and promoting equality in the workplace. Seek feedback from female colleagues, participate in diversity and inclusion training, and actively seek opportunities to learn from diverse perspectives.

Senior leaders supporting women

Gender disparity in corporate leadership within Australia is significant. The Workplace Gender Equality Agency[82] reported in 2024 that 32% of corporate boards in Australia have no female members, and only 22% of CEOs are women, highlighting the deep gender bias in organisations.

Only 7% of managerial roles are part-time, making it hard for women, who still hold the greatest responsibility for child-care, to balance work and family commitments. These figures show the urgent need for action to create an environment where women can thrive in leadership.

It's certainly possible for women to thrive in part-time roles by increasing their impact while reducing working hours. In her book *Solving the Part-Time Puzzle,* Belinda Morgan challenges traditional assumptions about part-time work. She demonstrates how a strategic approach can boost professional contributions and personal wellbeing.[83] Morgan encourages women to navigate career challenges and create fulfilling work-life balances by focusing on prioritisation, boundary setting and leveraging flexibility. This is a great book, full of practical insights for achieving success without compromising personal aspirations.

In my current part-time engineering role, I embody the principles outlined in *Morgan's book* by maximising my impact through strategic prioritisation and focus. Much of my time is dedicated to acting as a role model for women within the organisation, and coaching and mentoring female graduates. By balancing technical responsibilities with initiatives that support diversity and inclusion, I demonstrate how part-time professionals can contribute meaningfully to organisational culture while fostering personal and professional growth for others.

However, senior leaders are vital in driving this change by implementing policies promoting gender diversity and inclusion. Male leaders need to advocate for women, even when they are not present, by addressing behaviours and subtle boundary violations that hinder women's advancement.

Senior leaders make a significant impact by creating a workplace where everyone has equal opportunities. Their commitment to diversity drives real change and moves women into leadership roles, unlocking their full potential. The best action for any senior leader is to lead by example.

Identify high-potential women — Actively identify women who demonstrate talent, potential and leadership capabilities. Pay attention to women's achievements, contributions and performance and recognise their potential for future growth and success.

Create opportunities — Once high-potential women are identified, create opportunities for them to display their skills, talents and leadership potential. Nominate them for high-profile projects, assignments or leadership roles and advocate for their inclusion in key decision-making processes and discussions.

Provide visibility and exposure — Promoting women's achievements. Advocate for their recognition and ensure their contributions are acknowledged. Highlight their successes in meetings, presentations and discussions, and provide opportunities for women to show their expertise and leadership skills.

Remove barriers — Use your power to remove obstacles that hold women back at work. Support policies that promote gender equality, challenge bias and discrimination, and create a more inclusive and supportive environment for all.

Provide mentorship and guidance — Sponsor and mentor women by offering guidance, support and advice to help them succeed in the workplace. Provide mentorship, give feedback, coach and help women build their skills, networks and professional connections.

Advocate for promotion and career advancement — Support women's career growth by advocating for them for leadership roles and development opportunities. Highlight their qualifications and advocate for their advancement to senior positions within the organisation.

Personal strategies

To conclude this chapter I thought it would be useful to provide some personal strategies to handle challenges that may arise at work. Remember, we cannot control others or external situations; we can only control our reactions. This control starts with how we think about boundary violations. Managing these thoughts helps us respond better and protect our wellbeing.

Bias interruption techniques are strategies to identify and mitigate unconscious biases in real time, helping create a fairer and more inclusive environment. For example, asking for concrete evidence when someone makes an assumption encourages more data-driven decisions. I recommend the Jefferson Fisher podcast for simple, practical strategies to set boundaries, interrupt bias and shift your thinking.[84] His advice is both enjoyable and useful.

If quick retorts or one-line responses are not your strength, try strategies like rotating meeting roles (facilitator, note-taker, chairperson, etc.) to include diverse perspectives. My formal training in safety engineering has shown that using structured decision-making tools, like checklists, can reduce bias and reliance on gut feelings. These approaches help create a more equitable work environment.

Speak out against discrimination. Address biased language. Try these ways to respectfully challenge what you see.

> ***'I noticed that during the meeting, some language was used that could be interpreted as biased against women. I believe it's important for us to be mindful of our language and avoid perpetuating gender stereotypes in the workplace.'*

Chapter 8: Challenging Gender Bias

**'I've been reading about the impact of gender bias in the workplace, and it's been on my mind lately. I think it would be beneficial for us to have a discussion about how we can promote diversity and inclusion and address any unconscious biases that may exist within our team.'*

'I've noticed a few instances recently where gender bias may have influenced certain decisions or behaviours. I wonder if there's an opportunity for us to learn more about the effects of these biases and explore ways we can create a more inclusive environment for everyone.'

Professional Boundaries

A garden requires patient labour and attention. Plants do not grow merely to satisfy ambitions or to fulfil good intentions. They thrive because someone expended effort on them.

— Liberty Hyde Bailey [85]

Personal and professional boundaries serve distinct purposes in our lives. Personal boundaries protect our emotional wellbeing, defining how we interact with others in our private lives. On the other hand, professional boundaries establish the limits of acceptable behaviour and interactions within the workplace, ensuring mutual respect, productivity and ethical standards.

This chapter specifically addresses maintaining professional boundaries, focusing on strategies to navigate workplace relationships, manage expectations and foster a healthy, respectful professional environment.

Government support for gender equality

Developing professional boundaries is essential for women to succeed in their careers without compromising their values. The Australian Government's Department of the Prime Minister and Cabinet supports developing gender equality by addressing foundational gender attitudes and stereotypes.[86] It is critical to fostering a work environment where women can thrive. In 2022, it identified that abandoning prescriptive gender norms could grow Australia's economy by, on average, AU$128 billion a year.[87]

Therefore, helping women establish clear boundaries at work helps them navigate the challenges posed by implicit biases and current societal expectations. This can help them maintain their professional and personal integrity and values. By promoting gender equality and challenging stereotypes, women can create a professional space that respects their contributions and aspirations, ultimately leading to a more inclusive and equitable workplace.

Nurturing the garden

Setting professional boundaries is akin to tending a garden: both require consistent care and effort to truly thrive. Each boundary you establish and uphold is like nurturing a specific garden bed, demanding thoughtful attention and ongoing maintenance.

Chapter 9: Professional Boundaries

Gardens do not flourish solely because of ambitions or good intentions but because someone actively invests time and energy in their upkeep. So too, boundaries cannot succeed with a 'set-and-forget' mindset; they need to be regularly evaluated and reinforced. Thriving in the workplace requires intentional boundary setting and consistent effort.

Today's fast-paced and challenging workplaces offer opportunities and obstacles. Establishing and maintaining boundaries is central to women's success. This chapter discusses the importance of workplace boundaries and provides practical tips to help women navigate them. From creating a respectful and professional environment to balancing work and personal life, setting clear boundaries is essential for women who want to thrive in their careers.

Defining professional boundaries

Professional boundaries set clear expectations for behaviour, actions and interactions leading to respectful work environments.

Effective communication is essential, including using the correct language and tone to convey your message. Defining roles and responsibilities can prevent crossing boundaries or stepping into others' areas, ensuring clarity and teamwork. It is also important to balance work and personal time to avoid overworking and protect your boundaries outside work hours.

Maintaining clear boundaries with colleagues, supervisors, clients and stakeholders is key to professionalism and avoiding conflicts of interest. With the rise of flexible work since the pandemic, personal and professional boundaries are becoming more blurred, making it harder to separate work and personal life. Chapter Eleven goes further into this issue, looking at how changing work environments affect boundaries and offering tips on handling these shifts.

Although boundary-setting may seem simple, the reality is that violations still happen in workplaces for many reasons. As discussed in earlier chapters, managing these dynamics, especially across diverse teams and cultures, requires careful attention.

Personal boundaries in professional settings

Before discussing professional relationships, I want to clarify how challenging these can be, especially with flexible working arrangements. We now have a level of flexibility that we did not have before COVID-19. With Zoom and Teams calls from home, we see glimpses of people's personal lives beyond their professional roles. Flexible working arrangements have changed what hours we choose to work and how we prioritise our time. Your boss's or colleagues' priorities may not always align with yours, as we saw in the Chapter Five case study on Megan's school pick-up time. While flexibility is essential, it can sometimes create tension in professional relationships.

However, it is also worth noting that some aspects of work that were never genuinely professional were often accepted as 'just the way it was'. This mindset, which is especially prevalent in male-dominated industries, has allowed misogynistic and patriarchal

Chapter 9: Professional Boundaries

behaviours to persist as the norm. This makes it hard for women to assert their boundaries without fear of discomfort or risking their careers. Navigating male-dominated industries is challenging for women, but communicating assertively when a colleague's behaviour is unacceptable is critical.

Working in male-dominated industries

Women in male-dominated industries often struggle with setting boundaries due to the fear of being perceived as less committed to their work. This challenge is compounded by research from *The Gender Gap in Self Promotion,* which found that women tend to undervalue their achievements by at least 24%, even when they outperform men.[88] This tendency toward self-criticism not only hampers their confidence but also weakens their ability to assert boundaries, leaving them at a disadvantage in maintaining a healthy work-life balance and advocating for themselves in professional settings.

A 2023 survey of four thousand British adults shows that women more commonly report imposter syndrome than men. Around 53% of women experience imposter syndrome, compared with 37% of men.[89]

> Around 53% of women experience imposter syndrome, compared with 37% of men.

These feelings are particularly prevalent in professional settings, with many women reporting that imposter syndrome also affects other areas of their lives, such as education and social interactions. Interestingly, cultural factors may play a role, as the gender gap in imposter syndrome is more pronounced in Canda and the USA and Europe than in Asia.

The study also found that imposter syndrome often begins around age twenty-three for women, with 62% admitting they have rarely felt true confidence. Triggers include societal pressures to 'have it all', with one in five women citing this as a key cause and 44% feeling that constant comparison to others plays a role. Worryingly, only 25% of women have openly discussed their imposter syndrome, compared to 37% of men, and just 30% of women have actively tried to overcome these feelings.

While specific data on imposter syndrome among Australian adults is not readily available, given the cultural and societal similarities between the UK and Australia, as well as the statistics provided in Chapter Seven highlighting rising anxiety levels among young girls and women in Australia, it is reasonable to assume that similar percentages would likely apply. That suggests that imposter syndrome may be prevalent at comparable rates in both countries.

To address this, we need to change how women view themselves and for men to understand that women tend to be much harder on themselves. Women must also improve at balancing assertiveness with diplomacy to maintain relationships and protect their wellbeing.

Chapter 9: Professional Boundaries

A PERSONAL PERSPECTIVE

I struggled with imposter syndrome for a long time, constantly feeling the need to go above and beyond to prove myself. Over time, I realised that this drive led to cynicism, resentment and ultimately burnout, all due to the unrealistic demands I placed on myself, fuelled by my internal dialogue and lack of realistic boundaries. I even left jobs because the harder I worked, the more my male colleagues expected from me. Looking back, I can now see that I set the bar too high, creating these expectations myself, driven by my inner critic's relentless pressure.

After setbacks and personal growth, I have learned that setting boundaries is essential for balance and wellbeing. From talking with other women in male-dominated industries, I have heard comparable stories of challenges that their male colleagues often do not even realise exist. Whether self-imposed or externally received, we need to improve at setting realistic expectations, communicating boundaries and discussing our challenges with male colleagues.

Lack of respect for boundaries

Women in STEM-related or male-dominated fields frequently face more interruptions and boundary violations than their male counterparts, contributing to decreased productivity and increased stress. This contention is supported by research that found women faced more interruptions, resulting in fragmented work time and greater emotional exhaustion.[90]

Interruptions disrupt workflow, increasing the chances of mistakes and making it harder to regain focus. Beatriz Boavida from *WorkJoy* found that even brief interruptions can drastically raise error rates, with more than 90% of yearly productivity lost to distractions.[91] Many workers struggle to get even one to two hours of focused work each day. Boavida's study shows it takes about twenty-three minutes to refocus after a distraction, and 60% of people cannot achieve deep work without interruption. Even short interruptions, like email notifications or someone walking by, can triple task error rates. These findings highlight the importance of setting and respecting boundaries to avoid being overwhelmed, frustrated and having reduced productivity. Without managing these interruptions, your stress levels and productivity will suffer.

Boundary crossing impacts workplaces

There's a big gap between how much trust management thinks they have and the actual trust employees feel. The Edelman Trust Barometer 2024 report reveals that many business leaders overestimate the trust they have, which can hurt performance and employee engagement.[92]

Statistics from *TeamStage* show significant gaps in leadership quality and trust in organisations.[93] While 83% of companies see value in developing leaders, only 48% of employees rate their leadership as 'high quality', and 71% lack confidence in their leaders. This distrust lowers morale and productivity, as employees feel undervalued.

In Australia, trust is further strained by slow progress in women's leadership. Only 18% of C-level roles are held by women.[94] This figure has only improved by 1% in the last five years.[95] It reflects the ongoing inequality and gender biases that weaken trust in the workplace.

Organisations should focus on clear communication, inclusive leadership and dedicated support systems that prioritise employee wellbeing and growth to address these trust deficits. These strategies close the trust gap and create a more united and productive workplace.

> **Consistently crossing boundaries at work harms individuals and the organisation.**

Consistently crossing boundaries at work harms individuals and the organisation. It damages trust and reduces employees' sense of safety. When boundaries are repeatedly ignored, people feel disrespected, invalidated and vulnerable, which breaks down trust between colleagues and management, making communication and teamwork harder. It also leads to a toxic work culture, creating tension, anxiety and resentment. This increases conflicts, lowers morale and causes stress and burnout. When boundary violations are accepted, employees are more likely to leave, seeking workplaces where they feel valued and respected.

Employee turnover affects organisational stability

Employee turnover in Australia has a significant fiscal impact on organisations. An ELMO Software and Australian HR Institute survey found that the average cost to hire a new employee jumped from AU$10,500 in 2020 to AU$23,860 in 2021. That covers expenses like advertising, interviews and onboarding, but excludes the salary of the departing employee.[96] However, a PricewaterhouseCoopers (PwC) study shows the actual cost is much higher when considering team disruptions, loss of knowledge and reduced productivity.[97] For executive roles, costs rise even further. *Workable* reported it can cost an extra AU$14,936 per role and take up to ninety-four days to fill such positions.[98] This delay can increase staff workload, lower morale and disrupt business continuity.

These statistics highlight the need for strong employee retention strategies to avoid excessive turnover costs, especially when boundary-crossing behaviour is a factor. Therefore, organisations should invest in creating a supportive work environment to reduce turnover and retain valuable talent, saving the direct and hidden costs associated with losing employees.

Consistent boundary crossing can also result in significant legal and reputational risks for organisations. Employees who feel their boundaries are ignored may take legal action, resulting in costly lawsuits and damaging the organisation's reputation. A culture that tolerates such behaviour can attract negative attention from clients, customers and regulators, hurting the brand and credibility. This has been seen recently in Australia, where the four big accounting firms face criticism for how they treat employees.

Employees in these environments may also share negative views externally, further harming the company's reputation. As the saying goes, one bad story can overshadow many positive achievements. In the end, consistent boundary crossing harms an organisation's performance, culture and long-term success.

CASE STUDY: STRUGGLING WITH WORKPLACE CULTURE

An experienced scientist, Annette faced a challenging situation while working at a prestigious STEM-related university. Despite her hard work, expertise and education, she encountered a workplace culture dominated by a 'jobs for the boys' mentality. Within the university, there was a pervasive belief that success depended more on connections than on merit, fostering an environment of implicit and covert behaviour.

As Annette attempted to address the behaviour, she faced resistance from her colleagues and superiors. When she raised concerns about the unfair practices within the section, she was met with responses dismissing her concerns as overreactions or attributing her objections to jealousy. This lack of support and understanding left Annette frustrated and isolated, as her efforts to advocate for fairness and meritocracy went unheard.

Over time, the toxic workplace culture took a toll on Annette's self-esteem and judgment. Despite her best efforts to excel, make a meaningful contribution and provide quality research, she was continually overlooked and marginalised within the university.

> *Feeling disheartened and undervalued, Annette made the difficult decision to leave.*
>
> *In her exit interview, Annette chose not to cite specific instances of poor behaviour, recognising that her concerns had fallen on deaf ears during her tenure. Instead, she opted to depart gracefully, unwilling to burn bridges and risk further alienation. Although Annette's departure marked the end of her time at the university, her experience sheds light on the challenges individuals face when confronted with entrenched workplace cultures that prioritise connections over competence.*

This case study highlights that many individuals choose to leave gracefully and not call out bad behaviour, preferring to avoid drawing more attention to the torment they endured. However, it is not all doom and gloom. When someone decides to leave an organisation, they often gain a clearer understanding of the type of workplace they want, including the values, beliefs and behaviours they seek.

A PERSONAL PERSPECTIVE

I can totally relate to this experience. After leaving the military, I was initially unaware of the diverse types of cultures and organisations I could work for. I was naïve when choosing a role that aligned with my values and beliefs. In the seven years after I left the military, I changed jobs five times, thinking that I was the problem and was somehow broken. I now realise that part of the challenge was my undiagnosed ADHD and autism, coupled with the pervasive and sometimes toxic masculine culture of some of the various male-dominated industries that I worked in. All of which made it difficult for me to be authentic and fit in.

After much soul-searching to deeply understand my drivers and motivations. I have now found a place where I can contribute and feel valued. I am lucky enough to have the autonomy to work part-time for an engineering management consulting firm that allows me to nurture the next generation of engineers and work part-time in my company, coaching, mentoring and teaching leadership and cultural behaviours that support people and organisations. It has also allowed me to pursue what is dear to me and help others find their way to be their best through coaching and mentoring.

Drawing from my experience in job searching, career coaching and research, I provide a balanced perspective on high employee turnover based on who I have coached, where I have worked and the current market trends.

The positive impact of employee departures

High employee turnover is generally seen as a negative due to the costs and disruptions it causes. Yet, it can offer unexpected benefits that challenge conventional views. Turnover is an opportunity to introduce fresh perspectives, drive innovation and have employees align with organisational goals and values. Additionally, turnover can create space for internal promotions and professional growth, motivating remaining employees and enhancing the overall talent pool.

Under Jack Welch's leadership, General Electric regularly replaced the lowest-performing 10% of its employees. Supporters argued that this helped maintain the company's high performance and innovation.[99] This approach shows how strategic turnover can enhance talent and contribute to organisational success, especially when poor performers may have contributed to boundary-crossing behaviour.

Turnover can also motivate remaining employees by opening up opportunities for promotions and growth.[100] Seeing colleagues advance or leave for better roles inspires others to improve their performance and pursue their career goals, helping to create a more inclusive and dynamic culture. Additionally, turnover brings fresh perspectives and ideas. New hires bring innovative solutions and challenge existing practices, encouraging continuous improvement. This is especially valuable in industries like STEM, where staying competitive requires quick adaptation and creativity.

Handling workplace dynamics

Effectively managing workplace dynamics is vital to creating a healthy and productive work environment. At the heart of this is setting and maintaining professional boundaries, which help guide interactions, resolve conflicts and improve teamwork. Knowing how to handle workplace dynamics the right way is vital for success. Here's how one team handled it.

Chapter 9: Professional Boundaries

CASE STUDY: THE TALE OF A START-UP TECHNICAL TEAM

In a bustling start-up company of ten, the founders, Jeff and Jackie, were known as the dynamic duo. From the outside, it appeared that they led their team with zeal and enthusiasm. However, their interactions were fraught with tension, and discord beneath the surface rippled across the entire team.

Jeff, a seasoned marketer with a strong entrepreneurial spirit, tended towards micromanagement. While it wasn't always obvious, he often disregarded the boundaries of his colleagues during exciting and interesting projects. He frequently hovered over their shoulders, offering unsolicited advice and criticisms, undermining their autonomy and confidence. Despite their repeated requests for space and independence to meet client requests, Jeff persisted in his intrusive behaviour, dismissing their concerns as trivial.

Jackie was a fast talker with a boisterous demeanour and a reputation for her sharp tongue and abrasive communication style. When things didn't go her way, she frequently engaged in gossip and rumourmongering, spreading disharmony among team members and fostering a toxic work environment. Her lack of empathy for her colleagues and disregard for their feelings led to resentment and animosity.

Women in the team faced additional challenges arising from Jeff and Jackie's behaviour. Jeff's micromanagement disproportionately affected the three female team members when they tried to work collaboratively. They battled gender stereotypes when Jeff's micromanaging methods questioned their competence. His constant oversight exacerbated their self-doubt and hindered their professional growth. Meanwhile, Jackie's gossip often targeted the women as she wanted to be seen as the top woman. Her actions undermined their credibility and fostered a culture of mistrust.

The implications of Jeff and Jackie's boundary-crossing behaviour were intense. Team morale plummeted as colleagues felt stifled by Jeff's micromanagement and demoralised by Jackie's divisive behaviour. Communication breakdowns became rampant, hindering collaboration and productivity. Trust eroded as colleagues grew wary of sharing ideas or seeking help, fearing judgment or backlash.

As tensions escalated, the once-cohesive team splintered into factions, with cliques forming based on loyalty to either Jeff or Jackie. Productivity suffered as team members became preoccupied with navigating interpersonal conflicts and avoiding Jeff and Jackie's overbearing presence.

In the end, the negative impact of Jeff and Jackie's boundary-crossing behaviour reverberated throughout the entire team. High turnover rates ensued and a tarnished reputation damaged the firm's image. What originally started as a small firm trying to make it big through the founders' energy led to a toxic culture and blurred professional boundaries for all who worked there.

This example highlights the importance of establishing and respecting professional boundaries, particularly in supporting women to thrive in a healthy and productive work environment.

Chapter 9: Professional Boundaries

The impact of negative workplace behaviours

We know that poor workplace behaviours can reduce people's self-esteem and encroach on their boundaries. From my career experience, I've identified the following five common workplace behaviours that seem the most pervasive in male-dominated and STEM-related industries.

Poor communication

While this behaviour can come from malicious intent, it is more likely due to unclear objectives and task-focused thinking. As mentioned earlier, I've observed that the STEM community has a higher proportion of neurodiverse people, which may contribute to this issue. Poor communication can make sharing ideas with a team hard, leading to confusion. Your thoughts may seem clear to you but may not be so to others. Differences in communication styles, lacking confidence, language barriers, accents and assumptions about what others know lead to unclear communication between colleagues.

Ignoring diversity

We often dismiss different perspectives through ignorance or limited awareness of others' ideas. Human preference for interacting with like-minded individuals leads them to overlook diverse viewpoints. This can encourage groupthink, where dominant opinions are accepted without question, and promote authority bias, where people follow leaders without considering other ideas. These behaviours silence unpopular voices and weaken professional boundaries in the workplace.

Lack of empathy

Empathy, a cornerstone of effective human interaction, is broadly categorised into affective empathy and cognitive empathy. Affective empathy is the natural ability to resonate emotionally with others' feelings. This type of empathy is often seen as more instinctive and is commonly associated with interpersonal sensitivity. Many women are observed to exhibit strong affective empathy due to socialisation and nurturing behaviours encouraged during upbringing.

In contrast, cognitive empathy involves understanding and predicting others' emotional states by observing and mimicking social cues. Cognitive empathy is a learned behaviour shaped through experiences and interactions rather than instinctive emotional resonance.[101] This distinction is particularly relevant for neurodivergent individuals, who may not inherently lack empathy but might experience challenges developing cognitive empathy due to differences in social processing mechanisms.

The discussion of empathy often intersects with workplace dynamics, particularly in male-dominated and STEM environments. These settings may prioritise logic and devalue emotional expression, leading to a culture of emotional suppression. In such workplaces, individuals may believe emotions should be excluded from professional contexts, impacting team morale, trust and respect.[102] While this can affect anyone, it is sometimes more pronounced among neurodivergent individuals or those whose upbringing did not encourage emotional exploration.

Understanding and fostering cognitive and affective contributes to healthier team dynamics and greater inclusivity. Recognising that empathy is a skill to be developed provides an opportunity to improve interactions and emotional awareness across diverse professional environments.

Negative feedback

Negative feedback is often touted as the truth, but brutal honesty is really just brutal. It happens if we've had poor role models or influences or we copy the patterns of critical or harmful behaviour we grew up with. Some people with narcissistic or sociopathic tendencies possess a sense of superiority, where they believe they are always right and others' opinions are less valuable, causing them always to give negative feedback. CEOs and senior managers who do so negatively affect their organisations.[103]

Narcissism involves an inflated sense of self-importance, a need for constant admiration and a lack of empathy. It leads to negative, self-serving feedback aimed at reinforcing superiority, rather than helping others grow. Narcissistic managers may struggle to give constructive criticism, focusing more on self-promotion than their employees' development. This creates a toxic work environment where feedback is discouraging and not helpful. People with narcissistic or sociopathic traits often lack empathy, criticising others publicly or using hurtful language without considering its impact. This behaviour damages the workplace, breaks professional boundaries and erodes trust and respect among colleagues.

Conflict avoidance

Few people enjoy conflict. We avoid addressing it at work to maintain harmony and avoid confrontation. Fear of negative consequences, like poor performance reviews or limited career growth, also stops us.

Research from the Australian Gender Equality Government Organisation shows that women are generally socialised to prioritise harmony and avoid conflict more than men.[104] Gender stereotypes encourage women to be nurturing and less assertive, leading them to shy away from conflict to keep the peace. Doing so may inevitably affect their career progress and their ability to set boundaries or advocate for themselves at work.

McKinsey's *Women in the Workplace October 2023* report shows that microaggressions and biases discourage women from being assertive or aggressive, affecting their sense of safety and career growth.[105] This finding highlights the need for organisations to address these biases and create supportive environments where women feel confident asserting their boundaries. Some people may also see certain conflicts as too small to address, avoiding them to prevent tension or disruption. Avoidance leaves issues unresolved, weakening professional boundaries and harming team cohesion.

Positive workplace behaviours strengthen professional boundaries

As a coach, I am often asked how to be assertive without seeming aggressive, especially for women in male-dominated workplaces where communication can be misinterpreted. We might say one thing but mean another, leading to misunderstandings.

You've likely heard the saying, 'ASSUME makes an ASS out of U and ME'. Don't assume! If you are unsure of what someone means, use active listening. Try paraphrasing: 'What I heard you say was X. Did I get that right?' This approach ensures you understand them correctly and align with their intent.

I could write a whole book on this topic. Indeed, numerous books, podcasts, memes and videos highlight the differences between men's and women's communication styles. Instead of rehashing what many excellent speakers and researchers have said, I recommend Jefferson Fisher's podcast. He offers simple techniques to communicate your needs clearly without compromising your boundaries.[106]

Key practices encourage positive workplace behaviour that respects boundaries. Here are five basic practices to start with.

Effective communication

Promoting open and honest dialogue among team members fosters understanding, respect and better collaboration. That means clearly expressing your needs, expectations and limits while being mindful of how you communicate to ensure inclusivity. For example, if you prefer not to respond to emails after work hours, let others know your availability politely, clearly and firmly. Setting such expectations helps prevent misunderstandings and ensures boundaries are respected.

Additionally, avoid making assumptions about what others may already know and use appropriate language and tone in your interactions. Be mindful that some neurodivergent individuals may communicate directly without realising their tone might come across as abrupt or insincere. Instead of getting defensive, approach such situations with empathy and an open mind, seeking clarification if needed.

Active listening

Respecting diversity in the workplace involves more than acknowledging differences — it requires actively appreciating diverse perspectives, backgrounds and experiences while fostering an inclusive environment where everyone feels valued. This will only happen if you actively listen to what is being said and how it is communicated.

A key part of this process is understanding colleagues' views and concerns, showing empathy before responding and avoiding assumptions about their availability, requirements or understanding. Say you are in a meeting. Instead of presuming a colleague's ability to meet a deadline, listen to their concerns about conflicting priorities. By seeking to understand their unique challenges and collaborating on solutions, you demonstrate both empathy and respect for their perspective, creating a supportive and inclusive professional culture.

Constructive feedback

Deliver constructive feedback thoughtfully and supportively, focusing on actions rather than personal traits. This approach helps the individual understand what specific behaviours need improvement and creates an environment conducive to growth. Provide feedback based on clear, actionable examples rather than generalisations. Additionally, resolving conflicts quickly through open, honest discussions ensures that both the individual and the team can move forward positively.

Respecting personal time

Respecting personal time is essential for fostering a healthy work-life balance. Just because you work flexible hours, don't assume that others do as well. Do not expect colleagues to be available outside of standard working hours unless explicitly agreed upon beforehand. That includes avoiding scheduling meetings during lunch breaks and respecting team members' personal time.

Support time-off requests without imposing guilt or undue expectations. Reinforcing these practices demonstrates respect for personal time and creates a workplace culture where employees feel valued and balanced in their professional and personal commitments.

Maintaining professional distance

Be careful about how much personal information you share in your conversations at work. For example, mentioning weekend plans is okay, but discussing sensitive personal topics risks professional boundaries.

Setting boundaries is essential for creating clear rules for professional behaviour while respecting personal space, privacy and confidentiality. Team-building activities also help strengthen teamwork, develop a sense of belonging, and contribute to a positive and productive work environment.

CASE STUDY: JEFF AND JACKIE — TAKE TWO

Remember the scenario from earlier in this chapter? What happens to the outcomes if we change to a more constructive work ethic, where Jeff and Jackie, the dynamic founders, were known for their enthusiastic leadership and unwavering dedication to their team.

Jeff, an experienced marketer, demonstrated a commitment to effective communication by encouraging open dialogue among team members to foster understanding and collaboration. However, he occasionally struggled with crossing other people's boundaries. He often offered constructive feedback in a respectful and supportive manner but occasionally crossed the line into micromanagement. Despite this, Jeff showed a willingness to learn and adapt, actively listening to his colleagues' perspectives and concerns and seeking to understand before responding.

Meanwhile, Jackie exemplified respect for diversity by valuing and celebrating her team members' unique viewpoints, backgrounds and experiences. She was known for providing constructive feedback respectfully, focusing on behaviours or actions rather than personal attributes, and actively engaging in conflict resolution to address issues promptly and directly. Jackie occasionally faced challenges with empathy, particularly in high-pressure situations, leading to tension among team members.

Chapter 9: Professional Boundaries

> *Despite these occasional setbacks, the team remained resilient, buoyed by their commitment to setting boundaries and promoting team cohesion. Through team-building activities and a shared sense of purpose, they fostered a positive and inclusive work environment where everyone felt respected and heard. As a result, morale remained high, communication flourished and productivity soared.*
>
> *Jeff and Jackie's dedication to positive workplace behaviours ultimately strengthened the team and enhanced the firm's reputation. Their ability to navigate challenges gracefully and professionally underscored the importance of establishing and respecting professional boundaries to foster a healthy and productive work environment.*

What a change from the first scenario.

It is unrealistic to expect flawless performance from everyone all the time. Even on our best days, we are human and make mistakes. However, this case study shows we can significantly improve workplace morale and goodwill by being self-aware, recognising boundaries and knowing when and how they might be crossed.

Getting the right balance

Balancing teamwork with individual contributions is vital in maintaining a productive and respectful workplace. Encouraging positive workplace behaviours, as discussed earlier, requires creating a culture that fosters mutual respect and open communication.

In STEM industries, which are often characterised by a logical and systemising nature, you may encounter individuals who are direct or abrupt in their communication and lack strong social skills. These traits are not necessarily a reflection of rudeness or lack of empathy but rather the nature of the environment. It's important to consider this dynamic when striving for balance, ensuring that boundaries are respected without compromising the flow of ideas or collaboration.

Promote open communication and understanding of these characteristics to establish a more inclusive and supportive culture, allowing both group efforts and individual achievements to thrive.

The negative impacts of oversteppping boundaries

In the workplace, repeatedly crossing boundaries creates a toxic environment filled with tension and conflict. It lowers morale, with employees considering leaving or doing so, disrupting workflow and reducing productivity.

> Overstepping boundaries can have legal implications.

Overstepping boundaries can have legal implications, with cases of harassment, discrimination or confidentiality breaches. Lawsuits damage reputations. Constantly crossing boundaries destroys trust between colleagues, weakening the

Chapter 9: Professional Boundaries

professional relationships necessary for effective communication and teamwork.

Building on the ideas from Chapter Five, which explained how people react to boundary violations and the causes of conflict, such as past trauma and unhealthy coping strategies, let us now look at practical ways to set boundaries with colleagues, supervisors and clients who may overstep them, intentionally or not.

Effective communication for setting boundaries

Understanding human behaviour and distinct aspects of identity is necessary for fostering inclusive conversations. Mary-Frances Winters, a Diversity, Equity and Inclusion (DEI) expert and author of *Inclusive Conversations*, identifies eight conditions for such dialogues.[107] She emphasises that when setting boundaries at work, we must realise that not everyone is aware of their behaviour. Recognising this is crucial for creating a respectful and inclusive environment.

Navigating these differences often involves difficult conversations and possible resistance. The main goal when setting boundaries is to clearly communicate that, regardless of intent, your boundary has been crossed and you respectfully request a change in behaviour.

It is essential to understand that asserting boundaries may have negative consequences and support systems should be in place to handle them. While it is ideal for boundaries to be immediately respected, enforcing them can trigger reactions, so you must be prepared for potential challenges.

Managing difficult conversations

In my coaching sessions, handling difficult conversations is a common topic. I have sometimes sought advice from my coach for these situations. Whether with a supervisor, colleague, friend or partner, these conversations are loaded with fear of conflict, emotional discomfort and the potential impact on relationships. The anxiety often comes from worrying about misunderstandings, hurting feelings or damaging the relationship. While many resources are available to help with this, I have had the chance to share what I have learned with younger adults, with positive outcomes.

Chapter 9: Professional Boundaries

When preparing for a difficult conversation, consider these six essential points:

- **Stay calm** — Maintain your composure to ensure a constructive dialogue.
- **Plan what to say** — Prepare your points to communicate clearly and effectively.
- **Choose the right time and place** — Find an appropriate private and focused discussion setting.
- **Stay open-minded** — Be receptive to different perspectives and potential outcomes.
- **Set goals for the conversation** — To stay focussed, define what you hope to achieve.
- **Be prepared for any outcome** — Accept that the conversation may not go as planned and be ready to adapt.

For more advice on managing difficult conversations, Dr Ben Crosby, a professor of rhetoric and communication skills, offers valuable insights and strategies for effective communication.[108] He says that when communicating your boundaries, you may face negative reactions, such as defensiveness, anger or misunderstandings — particularly if others feel their actions were harmless or well-meaning. This can lead to feelings of guilt or self-doubt, especially when you worry about disappointing others or disrupting relationships.

There may also be fear of retaliation, particularly in professional settings with hierarchical structures, where you might fear losing favour or facing consequences for speaking up. To overcome these challenges, be clear and consistent when communicating your boundaries. Prepare for potential resistance, practice self-compassion and seek support from others who respect and understand your needs.

Whenever possible, approach conversations with curiosity and a desire to understand. Don't make assumptions about others' reasons or actions. Be mindful of any power imbalances. This mindset is key to understanding others.

Raising poor behaviour or boundary violations with colleagues or supervisors can be intimidating, but it is essential for a healthy work environment. If the behaviour persists, consider setting up a formal meeting to discuss your concerns directly. For instance, if a colleague frequently interrupts you during meetings, making it hard to share your ideas, reflect on possible reasons behind their behaviour, then ask rather than assume. You might be surprised.

NAVIGATING NEURODIVERSITY

Some neurodivergent people may interrupt without realising it because they process thoughts quickly and need to share them immediately. Understanding this can help you approach the conversation with empathy. However, not everyone has such challenges, so enter the conversation with curiosity about their behaviour. If the issue persists, here are some steps to help you handle the conversation effectively.

Planning for difficult conversations

Schedule a private one-on-one meeting

Let them know beforehand what the meeting is about. Preparation is only fair, especially if they are neurodivergent. Begin by expressing that your goal is to address the issue constructively and improve the working relationship. Use 'I' statements to explain how their behaviour has affected you personally and professionally. Be honest about how it has impacted your work and wellbeing. This approach encourages open communication and allows for a clear discussion about respecting boundaries within the team.

Provide specific examples

Clearly identify the behaviours that crossed your boundaries, using detailed examples to help illustrate your concerns. Focus on the behaviour itself, not the person.

For instance, you could say to the person who interrupted you:

'In yesterday's team meeting, I was interrupted several times while presenting my ideas, which made it hard for me to fully express my thoughts and left me frustrated. I think it is important that everyone has the chance to share ideas without interruption to keep the discussion fair and inclusive. I wanted to discuss this with you, so we can find a solution.'

If possible repercussions mean you are uncomfortable approaching the person who interrupted you, take it to your manager or the person chairing the meeting. This approach offers a constructive context without blaming the individual by focusing on the behaviour (interrupting) and providing a specific example.

Focus on solutions

Rather than focusing only on the problem, steer the conversation toward finding solutions. Suggest ways to address the behaviour and respect boundaries in future. For example, if a team member often interrupts during meetings, instead of just discussing the issue, propose solutions like a 'one-person speaks at a time' rule to ensure everyone can contribute. You could also suggest using a signal, like raising a hand, to indicate when someone wants to speak or setting a structured agenda where each person gets a turn to share their ideas.

Be open to feedback

Be open to feedback from your supervisor or colleague and listen to their perspective.

After hearing their feedback, you could say: *'Thank you for sharing your thoughts. I appreciate your insights and am open to any suggestions. I want to ensure we are aligned on the goals and expectations, and I'm committed to making adjustments to improve our results. Let's keep working together to find solutions.'*

This response shows your openness to feedback and your willingness to collaborate on improvements.

Chapter 9: Professional Boundaries

Maintain professionalism

To keep the conversation professional and avoid being defensive or aggressive. Focus on the facts and communicate respectfully. Acknowledge the other person's perspective and listen carefully. Respond calmly, even if you disagree. Use 'I' statements to share your thoughts without blaming anyone. Keep the focus on finding solutions and moving forward for a productive conversation and to maintain positive working relationships.

Follow up

After the conversation, show your commitment to resolving the issue by following up to ensure any agreements or action plans are carried out. Send a brief email summarising the key points and agreements made during the conversation. Thank them for the discussion, express your commitment to moving forward positively, and ask if further steps or adjustments are needed. Offering to help implement the agreed solutions keeps everyone aligned and shows your dedication to resolving the issue.

Choose your approach

If the boundary-crossing behaviour seems like a one-time or rare occurrence, you might choose a more casual approach. While I have shared strong***, medium** and soft approaches* for communicating your boundaries at work, always opt for the least harmful method. Choose from the following examples depending on the level of directness that will be most effective.

Here are some conversation starters to help begin the discussion:

*** 'Hello [Name], I've recently noticed a pattern of behaviour that I feel is important to address. When you [describe the behaviour], it impacts me in [explain your feelings]. I believe it's essential to maintain clear boundaries in our professional interactions, so I'd like to discuss how we can ensure that moving forward.'

** 'Hi [Name], I hope you're doing well. I wanted to bring up something that's been on my mind. I've noticed [describe the behaviour] lately, and I feel it's crossing a professional boundary. It's important to me that we maintain a respectful working relationship, so I'd appreciate it if we could [propose a resolution].'

** 'I'd like to address something with you, [Name]. Recently, I've noticed [describe the behaviour] happening, and it's been making me feel [explain your feelings]. I believe in clear communication and mutual respect, so I'd like to discuss how we can ensure that [suggest a way forward].'

* 'Hey [Name], I wanted to talk to you about something that's been bothering me. When you [describe the behaviour], it makes me feel [explain your feelings]. I value our working relationship, so can we find a way to [suggest a solution]?'

* 'Excuse me, [Name], I noticed [describe the behaviour]. You may not have realised it, but it made me feel [explain your feelings]. I'd appreciate it if we could [request a change in behaviour] to keep a positive work environment.'

It might feel daunting to discuss these issues, and you may worry that the suggested statements will make you seem too sensitive. If

Chapter 9: Professional Boundaries

that is a concern, try softening your approach while covering the three key points you want to address, as shown in Figure 13.

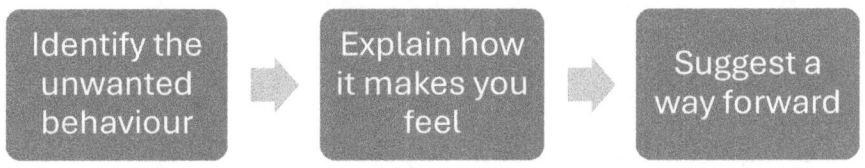

Figure 13: Boundary enforcing affirmation

Other strategies when work boundaries are crossed

There are other options besides using effective communication techniques.

Discuss the situation with an ally to decide if it is worth addressing or if another issue is the real cause. For example, someone upset about one issue (X) might vent about another issue (Y). Solving Y may offer temporary relief, but it will not address the root problem, which is X.

Recognise that when someone vents, they might not fully understand the root cause of their feelings or situation. Under the psychological safety amendment, the Australian Work Health Safety Act (WHS Act 2011) requires organisations to support both sides, using resources such as Employee Assistance Programs (EAPs), mental health professionals and trained counsellors.[109]

While this book offers simplified case studies and advice, real-life situations are often far more convoluted. Sometimes, simply being present, showing empathy and caring can make a significant difference. If further action is required, the following strategies will help you better define and protect your professional boundaries.

Actions to protect your boundaries

Direct communication***

As indicated above, speak directly to the person who crossed your boundary. Clearly and assertively explain your discomfort and which boundary was crossed. Use 'I' statements to express your feelings without blaming them. For example, 'I felt uncomfortable when you mentioned my personal life during the meeting. I prefer to keep personal matters separate from work discussions.'

Get comfortable saying no***

Learning to say no is vital for maintaining boundaries. Practice turning down tasks or meetings that do not fit your priorities. For instance, politely decline if you're asked to join a time-consuming committee that conflicts with your boundaries. If you find this difficult, here are some ways to decline without actually saying no.

> 'I appreciate the offer, but I have other commitments that I need to focus on right now.'
>
> 'That sounds interesting, but I'm currently prioritising other projects.'
>
> 'I'm flattered that you thought of me, but I won't be able to take this on.'

'I'm going to pass on this, but thank you for considering me.'

'I wish I could, but my schedule is fully booked at the moment.'

'This isn't something I can take on right now, but I can help you find someone who might be interested.'

'I'm not the best fit for this, but I appreciate you thinking of me.'

'I need to decline this time, but I look forward to future opportunities.'

If you struggle to say no or feel pressured to say yes, consider working with a coach or mentor for guidance. They will support you to reinforce your boundaries and encourage you when you feel guilty.

Document and report***

If the boundary violation continues after you have spoken to the person, document the incidents, including dates, times and details. Report the issue to a supervisor, HR or another appropriate authority. Share your evidence and ask for help in resolving the situation professionally.

Set clear boundaries**

Set clear boundaries for yourself and communicate them to your colleagues. Let them know what behaviours are acceptable or not in your interactions. For example, you might tell coworkers that you prefer not to discuss personal matters during work hours or need advance notice for schedule changes. If a colleague expects you to respond to emails after hours, politely let them know you are unavailable and will reply the next business day.

Recent changes to the Australian Fair Work Act 2009 (August 2024) give employees the right to disconnect outside work hours, addressing issues like after-hours email expectations. Just because someone works late does not mean others should. Set your expectations early to avoid misunderstandings. While working late may sometimes be necessary, it should not be the norm. Remember to uphold your boundaries, too.

Create clear structures for work**

Creating clear structures for work, including focused work times, helps maintain boundaries. Designate specific hours for uninterrupted tasks by blocking out time in your calendar and letting your team know you are unavailable for meetings or calls at these times. I started using the Agile project methodology to plan my monthly activities, which works well for any role. First, identify what needs to be done, then block out time to complete those tasks. Be realistic about how you spend your time and set boundaries for when others can request your time.

Delegate work when appropriate**

It might seem obvious, but women often take on more than our fair share of work, especially when our work and personal boundaries blur. To manage your workload, it is important to delegate tasks when possible. Trust your team to handle them. For example, if a junior team member can manage part of a project, let them take it on instead of overloading yourself. Delegating also means asking for help when someone has strengths you do not. From my experience, being honest about your abilities earns respect. It encourages your team to work independently, reduces bottlenecks and gives others the confidence to showcase their skills.

Develop self-compassion**

Treating yourself with the same kindness you would show a friend is key to coping with guilt and managing emotions. That's the finding of Kristen Neff, an expert in self-compassion.[110] Her studies show that self-compassion reduces stress and improves mental health, highlighting the importance of prioritising one's needs. Practising self-compassion builds resilience and develops a healthier mindset, making it a powerful tool for emotional wellbeing.

Seek support from allies**

Find trustworthy colleagues or mentors who can support and guide you through boundary issues. Share your concerns with them and get their advice on how to handle the situation. Having allies at work can help you feel validated and find constructive solutions.

Boundary adjustment*

For minor boundary issues with minimal impact, respond by adjusting your personal boundaries slightly to avoid confrontation. That might mean being flexible in certain areas or making minor changes to keep things peaceful.

Use nonverbal cues*

Use subtle nonverbal cues to set boundaries with colleagues. For example, keep a comfortable physical distance, avoid prolonged eye contact or gently steer conversations back to work topics. These subtle actions uphold your boundaries without the need for direct confrontation.

Self-care and coping*

Focus on self-care and coping strategies for mild boundary violations. Stress-relieving activities and keeping a healthy work-life balance will help you stay resilient and lessen the impact of these situations.

Leave the organisation*****

This one is last on the list because it is somewhat extreme. If frequent boundary violations at work are harming your mental health and wellbeing, it might be time to consider finding a new job. Think this through carefully. Don't make a rash decision you'll regret later. Before quitting, seek support, explore your options and consider the impact on your physical and mental health. Over the years, I have faced this choice several times and always sought advice and weighed my options carefully to prioritise my health and professional growth. Although leaving may not be ideal, your health and relationships should come first. Working for an employer or supervisor who does not value you can negatively affect your wellbeing for a very long time.

Chapter 9: Professional Boundaries

The strategies above offer many ways to handle boundary violations; choose your approach based on your comfort and the situation. While advocating for yourself is important, there are times when help is needed, especially due to power dynamics or workplace culture. In these cases, seeking support from allies in higher positions can be crucial to creating a supportive and inclusive environment.

Overcoming fear or guilt associated with asserting boundaries

Fear is a natural survival mechanism triggered by different situations. In Chapter Three, I explained how fear can be connected to past trauma or become a habit in certain situations. Along with fear, people may also feel guilt or shame, especially when dealing with boundary violations. Guilt can come from feeling obligated to please others or fearing disappointment. In contrast, fear may be linked to worries about conflict, rejection or adverse consequences of standing up for oneself.

> **When we fear judgment, failure or social exclusion, we worry we will be seen as unworthy.**

When we fear judgment, failure or social exclusion, we worry we will be seen as unworthy. The fear of being exposed as flawed can quickly transform into shame, particularly if our sense of identity is tied to success or acceptance. Past traumas may compound this fear, as current situations can trigger feelings of shame from previous experiences.

To wrap up this chapter, setting boundaries can be particularly challenging, as emotions and psychological factors such as fear, guilt and shame often complicate the process. You'll need strategies to manage these emotional responses effectively. Cultivating assertiveness skills is key to ensuring your boundaries are respected without compromising your personal wellbeing. For additional resources on learning assertiveness, refer to Appendix 5.

The Balancing Act

You can't have everything; you can't do everything; you can't be everything. But you can choose what is most important to you, and you can focus your energy and attention there.

— DEBORAH NORVILLE [111]

Achieving a healthy work-life balance is important for overall wellbeing — especially for working women who often manage multiple roles. Balancing work with personal and family commitments affects mental, emotional and physical health.

When work takes over personal time, it leads to stress, burnout and lower job satisfaction. On the other hand, good balance promotes better health, boosts productivity and brings fulfilment.

For working women, effective work-life balance strategies are key to thriving at work and in their personal lives.

Imagine your work-life balance as a seesaw, with you standing at the pivot point. In your younger years, with ample time and minimal pressure, maintaining equilibrium is effortless. However, life becomes more hectic as you grow older, possibly enter a relationship, start a family or care for others.

At the same time, advancing in your career brings additional responsibilities. Even without a family, commitments like after-work activities, team sports, volunteering, hobbies and self-care demand your attention.

As external demands arise, you begin shifting away from the pivot point. Initially, it's just a small step, but as pressures from work and personal life intensify, you find yourself running back and forth along the seesaw to keep from tipping too far in either direction. This constant movement highlights the challenge of maintaining balance amidst the ever-changing demands of your personal and professional life.

Identifying signs of burnout

The term 'burnout' is familiar to most of us. Far from the thrill-seeker who races around, leaving scorched roads and burning rubber, this type of burnout is far more insidious; it creeps up on you when you work too hard. It is the persistent feeling of exhaustion that lingers even after a good night's sleep (if you are lucky enough to get that much rest). This fatigue is often physical, emotional and mental, making it hard to muster the energy for tasks you once enjoyed.

Recognising the signs of burnout helps you act early to protect your wellbeing. You might notice a drop in work performance, trouble focusing or difficulty making decisions. Irritability, impatience or mood swings (like snapping at loved ones over trivial things) are warning signs. You may also feel detached or cynical about your work, leading to a lack of motivation or resentment toward your job, colleagues or friends. It can spill over into your personal life, causing you to withdraw from social activities. Physical symptoms like headaches, stomach issues or changes in sleep and appetite can signal burnout. If you know what to watch, you can take steps to regain balance and wellbeing.

A PERSONAL PERSPECTIVE

I was studying full-time for my engineering degree and navigating the demands of motherhood with my two daughters, aged 9 and 11, when I decided to take on the enormous task of running a three-day conference. My intention was to prove to my employer that I could do it all and that I was capable of excelling in every area of my life simultaneously. However, the reality was far from what I had envisioned.

I became increasingly snappy and irritable, and my patience thinned with each passing day. As forgetfulness crept in, I struggled to keep track of even the simplest tasks. Nights became a battleground for sleep, leaving me exhausted and unhappy with my lot in life. The constant pressure to excel in my studies, be a present mother, and demonstrate my capabilities at work and home was taking its toll.

The experience of burnout was overwhelming and all-consuming. As a woman in STEM, the pressures felt even more intense. The expectations to excel academically, professionally and personally were immense, and the struggle to balance these roles was daunting. The societal pressures and the internal drive to break barriers and defy stereotypes added another layer to the stress I was experiencing.

Burnout for women in STEM often carries unique challenges. In efforts to prove yourself in a male-dominated field, you might find yourself taking on excessive responsibilities, striving for perfection and neglecting self-care. The constant juggling of

Chapter 10: The Balancing Act

career aspirations and personal life leaves little room for rest and recovery, leading to a cycle of exhaustion and dissatisfaction.

My ordeal taught me that acknowledging my limits and seeking support were not signs of weakness but acts of strength and developing my resilience. It became clear that to thrive, I needed to prioritise self-care, set realistic goals and maintain a balance that respected my professional ambitions and personal wellbeing. Recognising the signs of burnout and proactively addressing them became essential steps in my journey towards a healthier, more fulfilling life.

Burnout is an all-too-common experience, and I've faced it multiple times. For those with ADHD, the tendency toward hyperfocus on stimulating tasks can heighten the risk of recurring burnout. Over the past fifteen years, I've become better at identifying warning signs and prioritising my health. However, burnout isn't exclusive to any particular group, and as women, we often downplay or hide the symptoms until reaching a breaking point. I cannot stress enough the importance of taking time off as a proactive measure to maintain balance, prevent burnout and sustain wellbeing.

Give yourself a break

Taking time off is essential for wellbeing, yet many employers and employees underestimate its value. A 2022 survey by ELMO Software, reported by Human Resources Director (HRD), found that 75% of Australian employees are not taking annual leave due to workload and financial pressures.[112] The report showed that 23% of workers had over twenty days of unused leave, and

13% had banked more than two months' worth. Baby boomers and gen X tend to have more accumulated leave than gen Z and millennials. This leads to widespread burnout, with over 50% of managers feeling exhausted. These findings stress the importance of taking time off to prevent burnout and improve productivity, creativity and mental health.

Regular breaks and vacations are key to rejuvenating and maintaining boundaries. Plan and communicate your time off in advance to manage your workload while you are away. I take three weeks off every six months to travel. If travel is not possible due to finances or family, even a weekend getaway or a date night with friends or your partner can help you unwind and relax. It does not need to be long or expensive; it just needs to allow you to recharge.

Your values are the key to balance

Your core values are the fundamental principles that guide your life and shape your beliefs, attitudes and behaviours. As highlighted in Chapter Two, reflecting on what values resonate with you and why they are meaningful is key to balancing work and personal life priorities. It is extremely difficult to purposefully determine your values without first identifying your priorities. Without this clarity, you

> You may be caught between what you want to do, what you should do and what others expect of you.

Chapter 10: The Balancing Act

may be caught between what you want to do, what you should do and what others expect of you.

Incorporating self-care into your routine is essential when striving to achieve and maintain a work-life balance and doing what you must. Women sometimes feel that taking time for ourselves is selfish, but this is a misconception. Self-care and selfishness are distinct concepts.

Self-care is about maintaining or improving your wellbeing to ensure a balanced mental, physical and emotional state, often considering the positive effects on those around you. Conversely, selfishness prioritises personal desires and needs at the expense of others, neglecting their feelings and wellbeing. Embracing self-care fosters a healthier, more supportive environment, whereas selfishness can strain relationships and create resentment. Understanding these differences is crucial as we identify our values and strive for a harmonious work-life balance.

Self-care is like tending to a garden. Each aspect of your wellbeing is a seed full of potential. When you nourish these seeds with healthy food, regular hydration and positive habits, they grow strong and vibrant, just like plants basking in the sunlight and enriched by fertile soil. Your garden thrives, blooming with beauty and resilience.

The Boundary Blueprint

However, the plants will wither if you neglect your garden, deprive it of water, allow weeds to take over and ignore the essential care it needs. Weeds of stress and exhaustion will choke the life out of your once-flourishing garden, leaving it barren and lifeless. Just as a gardener must consistently tend to their plants, you must continuously nurture yourself to cultivate a life of health, happiness and fulfilment.

There is, of course, a caveat: putting ourselves first every time is unrealistic and inconsiderate. As social beings, we thrive on relationships and cooperation. Constantly prioritising yourself can strain relationships and lead to resentment, damaging trust and support. Empathy, compassion and altruism are essential for personal fulfilment and moral integrity.

Most of us have encountered someone who seems always to put their needs and desires first. However, teamwork and collaboration are key in professional settings, and self-centred behaviour can harm team performance and workplace harmony. Good leaders balance looking out for themselves with supporting their team. Always prioritising oneself can hurt credibility and effectiveness. Cultural norms stress considering others; ignoring this can lead to isolation or conflict. Balancing self-care with concern for others is essential for healthy relationships, ethical behaviour and teamwork.

Work-life balance in STEM

As we've seen, women in STEM face unique challenges when setting career goals while balancing their personal lives. The lack of representation and visible role models in leadership makes it hard for younger women to see a clear career path. Although there has been progress, there are still too few women in high-level positions. Biases and stereotypes questioning women's abilities can also undermine their confidence, discouraging them from setting ambitious goals.

Balancing professional duties with personal or family commitments adds another layer of difficulty. Juggling these roles often leads to unclear priorities, making future planning harder. Additionally, the male-dominated culture in STEM can pressure women to conform to norms that do not match their values, causing dissatisfaction and unfulfilled goals.

Set goals for balance and boundaries

Master coach Michael Bungay Stanier shares a method for setting worthy goals that help maintain work-life balance and avoid burnout. He defines a worthy goal as thrilling, important and daunting. It excites you, pushes you to grow and benefits the community. His book *How to Begin: Start Doing Something That Matters* and the accompanying online course are worth checking out.[113]

To balance work and personal life, start by defining a goal that meets Stanier's criteria — for example, leading a major project at work that also promotes personal growth. Making your goals fulfilling and enriching reduces the chance of feeling overwhelmed.

What I appreciate about Stanier's method is that it focuses on committing to your goal by assessing your readiness and understanding the efforts needed. It encourages you to reflect on past habits to avoid repeating mistakes. Ensuring your goal is realistic and manageable is a positive step to avoiding over-commitment.

> Take small, manageable steps toward your goal.

Maintaining balance means you take small, manageable steps toward your goal. This helps you build momentum and make adjustments as needed. If you are unsure about doing it alone, get help from a coach or surround yourself with supportive people for encouragement. Regular self-reflection is part of the process. By regularly assessing your progress and aligning your goals with your values, you have a greater chance of preventing stress and burnout.

> ## PERSONAL REFLECTION
>
> *I achieved a personal worthy goal in 2010 by organising the inaugural Australian and New Zealand Institute of Electrical and Electronic Engineers (IEEE) Student Congress (ANZSCON2010). As the inaugural chair, I led an event that brought together like-minded students from across Australia and New Zealand to showcase their university projects and network with peers. This goal was worthy because it served a purpose greater than my own, benefiting many engineering students by fostering connections and sharing knowledge.*
>
> *The experience was thrilling because it was the first event of its kind, allowing us to create something entirely new. Although we had to adhere to a budget and rules set by the IEEE Victorian branch, we enjoyed the freedom to design an impactful event. Organising ANZSCON gave me and the student committee a strong sense of purpose, knowing we were contributing to the future of our fellow students.*
>
> *It was also daunting. We invested considerable time and resources into promoting the event, although we were unsure if it would succeed. This challenge motivated us to stay focused and committed, resulting in a successful congress that left a lasting impact on the participants and set a precedent for future events.*
>
> *The conference was an enormous success and is still being run by like-minded students who also believe in the worthy original goal I set.*

Setting goals

Setting goals is like climbing a ladder: each rung represents a step toward your ultimate goal. The climb becomes exhausting and overwhelming if the rungs are spaced too far apart. Similarly, setting large goals without breaking them into smaller steps makes achieving them much harder. Mini goals provide necessary support and milestones, making the journey more attainable.

You can set meaningful goals for work and personal life using methods that fit your needs. Setting worthy goals is key to professional success, maintaining boundaries and balancing life. In demanding, male-dominated fields, clear, attainable goals help you avoid sacrificing one aspect for the other.

Using goal-setting techniques, you can create a structured plan that aligns with your long-term vision. Breaking down larger goals into smaller tasks makes the process less overwhelming and more achievable — much like climbing a ladder with closely spaced rungs. Establishing personal goals that foster self-care, personal growth and leisure prevents burnout and promotes a healthier lifestyle. Worthy goals create a roadmap that respects your professional ambitions and personal needs, enabling you to thrive in all areas of your life.

Different goal-setting methods

Goal-setting can be incredibly beneficial for gaining a clearer understanding of your values and belief systems, as well as identifying your career-related goals. When you understand your goals, you gain insight into where your boundaries lie and how to enforce them, ensuring your goals are not compromised. By aligning your objectives with your core values, you can create a balanced and fulfilling path forward, maintaining personal and professional integrity.

One book that has helped me better understand people and their personalities is *Surrounded by Idiots* by Thomas Erikson.[114] Erikson divides personalities into four types — Red, Yellow, Green and Blue — each with unique traits. Understanding these types can improve how individuals approach goal setting, allowing coaching strategies to be better tailored to their needs.

Aligning goal-setting methods with your personality type will help you better understand your values, identify career-related goals and achieve long-term success. Understanding people's personalities and how they set boundaries (and also goals) offers a path to navigate interpersonal relationships in various contexts, including the workplace.

Product-related goals focus on achieving specific outcomes, such as publishing a research paper in a peer-reviewed journal within a year. Process-related goals emphasise the steps and behaviours needed to reach an objective, like dedicating two hours daily to conducting experiments and analysing data for a science-related project. Recognising the distinction between these types of goals helps balance the focus on desired outcomes and the necessary processes.

For instance, a Red personality, who is results-oriented and driven, might thrive with SMART goals that provide clear, measurable outcomes. A Yellow personality, who is enthusiastic and people-oriented, might prefer the CLEAR method, which focuses on energising and personally meaningful goals. Green personalities, valuing stability and relationships, could benefit from the GOAL method, integrating growth and learning opportunities. Blue personalities, analytical and detail-oriented, might favour WOOP goals, focusing on planning and overcoming obstacles. I'll explain each of these in more detail soon. That is not to say you can't use any goal-setting methods; it just offers some variety based on your style.

While I am a great fan of Michael Bungay Stanier's work, there are many ways to approach goal-setting. I use the following methods with my coaching clients, based on whether the goal is product or process-related, aligned to their personality style and how they prefer to approach their goal-setting activities.

SMART

The SMART method (Specific, Measurable, Achievable, Relevant and Time-bound) helps ensure your goals are clear and attainable within a set timeframe. For example, a SMART goal could be to learn a new programming language within six months.

Specific — Define your goal clearly and precisely. It should answer the who, what, where, when and why.

Measurable — Ensure that your goal is trackable and measured. This will help you stay motivated and track your progress.

Achievable — It must be realistic and attainable, considering your resources and constraints. It should challenge you but still be within reach.

Relevant — It must be important and relevant to you. It should align with your values and long-term objectives.

Time-bound — Set a deadline for your goal. This will create a sense of urgency, to stay focused and on track.

Who is it for?

This method is particularly beneficial for individuals who thrive on structure and clarity. This method is ideal for:

Analytical thinkers who prefer clear, detailed and logical planning. The specificity of SMART goals aligns well with the precision required in STEM disciplines.

Data-driven professionals who value measurable outcomes and need concrete evidence of progress. The measurable aspect of SMART goals ensures they can track their achievements quantitatively.

Realistic planners who appreciate setting realistic and attainable goals. The achievable component helps professionals set practical targets based on their resources and constraints.

Goal-oriented individuals who are focused on achieving specific outcomes within a set timeframe. The time-bound nature of SMART goals maintains motivation and ensures deadlines are met.

Detail-oriented workers who are meticulous and value comprehensive planning. The structured approach of this method ensures that every aspect of the goal is well thought out and planned.

SMART goal setting helps individuals and teams track progress and stay focused on goals; however, it can be rigid and hard to adjust to unexpected changes. SMART goals work best with product-focused tasks and for those who prefer clear, measurable and time-bound goals, offering clarity and accountability.

CLEAR

The CLEAR framework (Concise, Liveable, Energising, Achievable and Relative to self) highlights creating practical and inspiring goals, making it ideal for dynamic environments.

A CLEAR goal might involve setting a concise objective that fits seamlessly into your daily routine (liveable), energises you with its relevance and potential impact, is realistically achievable, and is tailored to your strengths and aspirations (relative to self). For example, you might aim to complete a specific research project that aligns with your passions and skills, provides a sense of accomplishment, and can be integrated smoothly into your existing commitments.

This approach ensures that your goals are attainable, motivating and personally meaningful.

Concise — Define your goal clearly and briefly. A concise goal is easy to remember and stay focussed on.

Liveable — Ensure the goal fits well into your daily life and routine. It should be practical and not cause excessive stress or disruption.

Energising — Choose a goal that excites and motivates you. It should give you energy and enthusiasm.

Achievable — Set a goal that is realistic and attainable, given your current resources and constraints. It should challenge you but still be within reach.

Relative to self — Make sure the goal is personally meaningful and relevant to your interests and values. It should be about your growth and improvement.

Who is it for?

The CLEAR goal-setting method is particularly beneficial for individuals who prefer structured yet flexible approaches to their work. This method would be ideal for:

Concise thinkers who value clear, succinct goals that are easy to understand and communicate. Precision is critical in STEM, and the CLEAR method helps maintain focus without unnecessary complexity.

Work-life balancers who seek to integrate their professional goals with their personal lives effectively. The 'liveable' aspect ensures that goals are realistic and manageable within their lifestyle, preventing burnout.

Motivated innovators who need energising and inspiring goals to maintain high levels of motivation and innovation. This method ensures that their objectives are exciting and engaging, keeping their passion for their field alive.

Pragmatic achievers who appreciate goals that are challenging yet achievable. The CLEAR method balances ambition with practicality, making it easier to set realistic milestones that are within reach.

Self-reflective learners who value personal growth and alignment with their core values. The 'relative to self' component encourages setting goals that are meaningful on a personal level, fostering a deeper connection to their work and personal development.

This goal-setting style may not work as well for those who prefer collaborative goal-setting, as it is more individual-focused. By emphasising clarity, realism and personal relevance, the CLEAR approach ensures goals are attainable and closely connected to one's values and daily life.

GOAL

The GOAL method (Growth, Opportunity, Action and Learning) focuses on personal and professional development through continuous learning and seizing opportunities. For example, setting a goal to publish a research paper involves seeking opportunities for collaboration, taking actionable steps each week to conduct experiments and gather data and continuously learning from successes and setbacks. You can systematically identify and achieve your professional and personal aspirations by leveraging these methods.

Growth — Identify how achieving this goal will contribute to your personal and professional development. Consider what skills or knowledge you will gain.

Opportunities — Recognise the opportunities that achieving this goal will create for you. Think about how it can open new doors or lead to further achievements.

Actions — Determine the specific actions you will need to take to achieve the goal. Break it down into manageable steps.

Learning — Reflect on what you will learn during the process of achieving the goal. This includes skills, knowledge and experiences.

Who is it for?

This goal-setting framework is particularly beneficial for dynamic individuals who continuously seek personal and professional development. This method is ideal for:

Continuous learners who are committed to ongoing education and skill development. The learning aspect of GOAL ensures that they are constantly improving and staying current in their field.

Opportunity seekers who are proactive in identifying and seizing new opportunities. This framework encourages them to look for growth possibilities and leverage them for career advancement.

Action-oriented professionals who are driven by taking tangible steps toward their objectives. The action component of GOAL aligns with individuals who prefer to make steady progress through well-defined actions.

Growth-minded individuals who focus on personal and professional growth. This framework supports their desire to expand their capabilities and achieve new milestones.

Strategic planners who appreciate a structured approach that integrates growth, opportunities, actionable steps and learning. This method allows them to strategically plan their career path with a focus on holistic development.

This approach focuses on learning from experiences and encourages a flexible, adaptable mindset. However, it can be time-consuming and needs regular adjustments to keep up with changing goals. The GOAL framework works best for people focused on personal growth who like a structured but flexible way

Chapter 10: The Balancing Act

to set goals, helping them seize new opportunities and improve their skills.

If you are new to goal setting, consider working with a coach or mentor to get the most out of it. Understanding the strengths and weaknesses of each method helps you choose the best one for your personality and goals, allowing you to achieve your career goals while staying true to your values.

WOOP

Finally, the WOOP method (Wish, Outcome, Obstacle and Plan) encourages you to envision your desired outcome and identify potential obstacles, fostering resilience and strategic planning. For instance, if you wish to lead a research project, you would visualise the successful completion, acknowledge challenges like resource constraints and create a plan to overcome them.

Wish — Identify a meaningful goal or wish. It should be something you genuinely want to achieve and can realistically work towards.

Outcome — Visualise the best possible outcome of achieving the wish. Think about how you will feel and what the positive results will be.

Obstacle — Identify the main obstacles that stand in the way. These could be an internal obstacle (like procrastination or fear) or external ones (like a lack of resources).

Plan — Create a plan to overcome these obstacles. This part involves an 'if-then' statement that helps you prepare for the challenges.

Who is it for?

This goal-setting method is particularly beneficial for individuals who are reflective and process-oriented. This method is ideal for:

Reflective thinkers who benefit from introspection and a deep understanding of their motivations and potential challenges. WOOP encourages a thorough analysis of desires and obstacles, aligning well with reflective personalities.

Problem-solvers who excel in identifying potential hurdles and developing strategies to overcome them. WOOP's focus on anticipating obstacles and planning solutions caters to those with strong problem-solving skills, which are vital in STEM.

Realistic planners who prefer setting realistic and achievable goals. WOOP's emphasis on understanding and planning for potential obstacles ensures that goals are practical and attainable.

Process-oriented professionals who value the journey towards achieving a goal as much as the end result. WOOP's structured approach aligns with those who appreciate detailed planning and continuous progress assessment.

Self-motivated individuals who are driven by personal growth and self-improvement. WOOP's focus on internal motivations and planning helps self-motivated individuals stay committed to their goals.

This approach helps individuals plan for challenges and create strategies to overcome them. However, it may not suit those who prefer a more direct, action-based approach, as WOOP involves reflection and detailed planning. It works best for process goals and people who excel in thoughtful goal setting, helping them consider their wishes, outcomes, obstacles and plans.

Strategies to help maintain work-life balance

Below is a list of strategies to help you identify your values and priorities to maintain a healthy work-life balance. Each strategy includes an example to demonstrate how you can enact them, along with the challenges you may face and tips to overcome these obstacles.

Set clear goals

As described above, defining short-term and long-term goals for your career and personal life is important. Make sure these goals match your core values and priorities. Many people find this step challenging, but it is key to having a successful and fulfilling career. Without clear goals, you may end up drifting through your professional life without direction.

Challenge — Many people struggle with defining clear goals due to a lack of direction or fear of failure.

Example — Working as a lab scientist, set a short-term goal to master a new laboratory technique within six months and a long-term goal to lead your own research project within three years.

Tip — Break down your goals into smaller, manageable tasks, and regularly review and adjust them as needed. Seek mentorship and support from colleagues to stay motivated and on track.

Evaluate time usage

Track how you spend your time over a week or month to spot areas for improvement. Notice which activities drain your energy and which ones make you feel good. Many say they do not have enough time, but we all have the same amount — it is about what you prioritise and why. Knowing your values helps you focus on what matters to you, rather than what others expect.

Challenges — It can be difficult to recognise how time is being wasted or to change long-standing habits.

Example — Working as an engineer, keep a detailed log of your daily activities for a month to identify energy-draining tasks and more fulfilling activities.

Tip — Use time management tools and apps to track and analyse your activities. Prioritise tasks based on their alignment with your core values and delegate or eliminate less important tasks.

Create boundaries

Establishing clear boundaries between work and personal time is essential. To ensure respect, communicate these boundaries to your employer, colleagues and family. Knowing your values helps you set effective boundaries, making it easier to allocate time for work and personal activities.

Challenge — Setting and maintaining boundaries can be challenging due to external pressures and internal guilt.

Chapter 10: The Balancing Act

Example — As a woman with school-aged children working, establish specific work hours and communicate these boundaries to your employer, colleagues and family members.

Tip — Be assertive and consistent in enforcing your boundaries. Schedule personal time as you would important meetings and practice saying no to additional commitments that do not align with your priorities.

Flexibility and adaptability

Understand that your priorities may change over time due to personal or work circumstances. Stay flexible and adjust your plans as needed. Many people feel overwhelmed by too many tasks, but they are often not adapting to what truly needs to be done. They may stick to old habits instead of being open to change. If you cannot do it all, consider other options, like asking for help.

Challenge — Adapting to changing circumstances can be difficult, especially when it requires deviating from established routines or plans.

Example — As a woman working, if a family member falls ill, sometimes it is expected that you are the one to take care of them. Take time to reassess your workload and delegate tasks to team members while adjusting your schedule to provide necessary support at home.

Tip — Regularly review and adjust your priorities and plans to accommodate changes. Stay open-minded and creative in finding solutions, and do not hesitate to ask for help when needed.

Leverage support systems

We often hold ourselves back by not delegating. Use support systems like family, friends or colleagues. You do not have to do everything yourself. Nobody needs to be a martyr; you cannot always handle everything alone. Ask for help when needed — it helps you manage better and makes others feel appreciated.

Challenge — Many people feel reluctant to ask for help due to fear of appearing weak or burdensome.

Example — It can be hard for women to delegate tasks as they feel that they have to be able to do it all. Enlist family help with household responsibilities and engage in professional networks for support.

Tip — Build a strong support network and communicate your needs clearly. Remember that asking for help is a strength, not a weakness, and can enhance your efficiency, resilience and wellbeing.

Prioritise self-care

When feeling overwhelmed, take time for self-care. Set aside time each week or daily for activities that support your physical, mental and emotional health. This keeps your energy and resilience strong. Unfortunately, self-care is often the first thing we neglect when we do not understand what motivates us. That is why knowing your values is so important.

Challenge — Self-care is often the first to be neglected due to busy schedules and competing demands.

Example — Integrate daily self-care practices such as taking a lunch break to go for a walk, meditating in the morning or attending a yoga class in the evening.

Tip — Schedule self-care activities as non-negotiable appointments. Reflect on your core values and recognise the long-term benefits of maintaining your physical, mental and emotional health.

Seek feedback

If you are unsure of your values, ask trusted friends, family or mentors for insights on your strengths and areas to improve. Be cautious of their motives; don't seek other opinions if they do not have your best interests at heart. A coach or mentor can be beneficial, as they offer unbiased advice and insights that others may not provide.

Challenge — Seeking feedback can be intimidating due to fear of criticism or appearing vulnerable.

Example — Ask your boss for feedback on your recent project, focusing on areas such as coding practices and project management skills.

Tip — Be specific in your requests and approach feedback sessions with an open mind. Use feedback to make actionable improvements and seek clarification when needed.

Self-reflection

After getting feedback from others, take time to reflect on what truly matters to you in your work and personal life. Think about what brings you joy, fulfilment and purpose. Journaling can help with this reflection by offering clarity and revealing feelings you might not have noticed before.

Challenge — Finding time for self-reflection can be difficult amid busy schedules.

Example — Set aside time each week to reflect on your experiences, challenges and achievements in a journal.

Tip — Make self-reflection a regular habit by scheduling it into your routine. Use prompts to guide your reflections and gain deeper insights into your values and goals.

In 2013, one of my coaches had me write a letter to my future self, identifying what I wanted to accomplish in the following twelve months, how I would feel and what I would say to myself upon achieving those goals. He then took the letter (without reading it) and mailed it to me a year later. I still have that letter and am amazed at how far I have come. Journaling can have a similar impact. When you reflect on what you wrote last week, last year, or even a decade ago, you can see how much your life evolves.

Regularly reassess

Journaling helps you track progress and notice any changes in your life. Periodically reassess your priorities to ensure they still match your life goals and align with your values. As people influence you, ongoing evaluation lets you adjust and stay balanced while being true to your evolving self.

Challenge — Ongoing reassessment can be overlooked due to complacency or resistance to change.

Example — Periodically review your journal entries to identify shifts in your values and priorities, ensuring they align with your current life goals.

Tip — Set regular intervals, such as quarterly or biannually, to reassess your goals and priorities. Stay open to making necessary adjustments to maintain alignment with your evolving self.

Recognise, too, how people in your life influence your values and priorities. Colleagues, mentors or personal relationships can shape your perspective. For example, a new mentor might inspire leadership, or a supportive partner may help you balance work and personal life better.

Regularly reviewing and adjusting your goals based on your changing values can keep your career and personal life balanced and fulfilling. This helps you stay true to yourself and aligned with your long-term goals.

Mindfulness practices

To boost self-awareness and decision-making, try mindfulness practices like meditation, walks or yoga to stay grounded. Mindfulness helps you manage emotions better, stay calm in tough situations, reduce stress and improve overall wellbeing by focusing on the present without judgment.

Challenge — Maintaining consistent mindfulness practices can be difficult due to a busy schedule and competing demands.

Example — Start your day with a 15-minute meditation session and take mindful walks during lunch breaks to stay grounded and focused.

Tip — Integrate mindfulness practices into your daily routine, even if only for a few minutes at a time. Use apps or join classes to help maintain consistency and remind yourself of the long-term benefits of reduced stress and improved emotional regulation.

By implementing these strategies and overcoming the associated challenges, you can effectively identify your values and priorities, achieving a healthier and more balanced work-life dynamic.

Chapter 10: The Balancing Act

 Guiding questions

Reflect on the following questions to clarify where your focus should be. For a more detailed assessment of each topic, refer to Appendix 6 at the end of the book.

Goal setting

1. What are your short- and long-term goals in your career and personal life? What methods have you used to identify and track these?

Time management

2. How do you track how you spend your time over a week or month?
3. How accurately do you estimate the time required to complete your tasks?

Boundary creation

4. Do you check work emails or think about work during your personal time?
5. What steps can you take to avoid overcommitting to work or personal obligations, which can lead to burnout?

Flexibility and adaptability

6. How do you typically respond to unexpected changes or challenges in your work or personal life?

7. What strategies do you use to handle unexpected interruptions or changes to your schedule?

Support systems

8. How often do you delegate tasks to others in your professional and personal life?

9. Who are the key members of your support system, and how do you utilise them?

Self-care

10. What changes can you make to your daily routine to enhance your overall wellbeing and satisfaction with your work and personal life?

11. How do you ensure that self-care remains a priority, even during busy times?

Feedback and self-reflection

12. How do you seek feedback on your strengths, weaknesses and areas for improvement?

13. When can you schedule regular check-ins or feedback sessions with your colleagues or mentors?

Reassessing values

14. How do you track your progress in aligning your actions with your values over time?

15. What core values are most important to you personally and professionally?

Chapter 10: The Balancing Act

Mindfulness practices

16. What mindfulness practices do you engage in to enhance self-awareness and decision-making clarity?

17. How can you incorporate mindfulness into your daily routine to enhance your focus, reduce stress and improve your work-life balance?

Reflect on your answers to notice areas needing more attention and make adjustments for better work-life balance. Don't be surprised if you struggle to answer — that is normal. A coach can help you gain clarity and find areas for improvement, offering valuable support for a more balanced and fulfilling life.

Digital Boundaries

*You cannot pour from an empty vessel,
you must take care of yourself first.*

— Eleanor Brown

Time has become an invaluable currency in the current climate of digital technology, where constant connectivity and rapid information exchange are the norm. Managing your workload effectively and avoiding burnout requires a strategic approach to investing this precious resource.

I agree with psychologist Daniel Goleman, who wrote, 'We need to re-create boundaries. When you carry a digital gadget that creates a virtual link to the office, you need to create a virtual boundary that didn't exist before.'[115]

With endless notifications, emails and tasks vying for our attention, it is easy to feel overwhelmed and overextended. This chapter focuses on practical strategies for managing digital boundaries, helping you prioritise screen time, balance online and offline tasks, and maintain a healthy relationship with technology. By learning how to set limits on digital engagement, manage notifications and create tech-free zones, you can ensure productivity while avoiding burnout. These techniques will empower you to take control of your digital habits, ensuring they support, rather than hinder, your wellbeing and energy levels.

Communication in the digital age

Communication is both instant and constant in the digital age, keeping us connected globally. For women in STEM, this brings opportunities and challenges. Recent technologies, such

Chapter 11: Digital Boundaries

as AI-driven tools and virtual reality meetings, will change how we collaborate and communicate. While these tools boost productivity, they also make it harder to maintain boundaries, especially in a demanding field like STEM. The constant flow of notifications and the pressure to respond immediately can blur the line between work and personal life.

To address this, set clear boundaries. For example, designate specific times to check work emails and let colleagues know when you are available. Use 'Do Not Disturb' or 'Focus Mode' to avoid interruptions during personal time. Separating work and personal accounts can also help create a clearer divide, making it easier to switch off from work. By managing your digital interactions and setting expectations, you can maintain a healthier work-life balance, protect your wellbeing and thrive professionally and personally.

The positive impact of digital technology

Digital technology has significantly influenced mental health. On the positive side, it provides easy access to resources like online therapy, support groups and wellness apps offering mindfulness, stress management and mental health tracking. These tools help people manage their mental health and seek support. Social media and online communities also create a sense of belonging, especially for those who feel isolated.

> Take small, manageable steps toward your goal.

Digital tools save time by streamlining tasks like project management and scheduling, reducing stress from juggling multiple responsibilities. This frees up time for research, innovation and professional development. Learning has also become easier with online courses and webinars, allowing people to stay updated with the latest knowledge and advancements, supporting lifelong learning and career growth.

Organisations increasingly use human-centred AI to make user lives easier by creating tools that boost productivity and wellbeing. For example, AI can personalise learning by offering tailored recommendations and automating tasks, giving employees time to focus on more creative and complex tasks.

Human-centred AI can provide accessible mental health support, with chatbots and virtual therapists to provide quick assistance.

CASE STUDY: WORKING SMARTER BY EMBRACING DIGITAL TECHNOLOGY

Michelle, a middle-aged executive in the tech industry, was initially overwhelmed by the rapid advancements in digital tools. However, she was determined to stay ahead and manage her workload more efficiently, so she decided to embrace these modern technologies. Michelle started by integrating ChatGPT into her daily routine. It quickly became her go-to tool for drafting emails, generating reports and brainstorming ideas. This tool saved her countless hours and enhanced the quality of her work with its insightful suggestions.

Chapter 11: Digital Boundaries

> *She also delved into Power BI, a powerful data visualisation tool. By upskilling herself through online courses and tutorials, Michelle learned to create dynamic dashboards that provided real-time insights into her projects. This newfound capability allowed her to make data-driven decisions swiftly and accurately, significantly improving her team's performance.*
>
> *Leveraging these tools meant Michelle could automate repetitive tasks and streamline the processes, which freed up time to focus on strategic planning and innovation. She no longer felt the constant pressure to be always 'on' and could set clear boundaries between her work and personal life. This smart approach to work helped her avoid burnout and maintain a healthier work-life balance.*
>
> *Embracing digital technology transformed Michelle's work life. She became more productive, efficient and less stressed. Michelle set a powerful example for her colleagues by working smarter, not harder, demonstrating that embracing digital tools can lead to greater success and wellbeing.*

There is a rider to this case study. While digital tools and AI can be helpful, they should be used carefully. Relying on AI to save time, especially when you are overwhelmed, can be risky. AI may produce results that seem correct but contain errors or lack context, especially if you are unfamiliar with the topic. These mistakes can hurt your work's credibility. When stressed or overworked, it is easy to miss these flaws, leading to serious issues. Therefore, AI should always be treated as a supplementary tool, and its outputs should be carefully reviewed and validated.

The negative impact on mental health

Constant connectivity and information overload from digital technology can harm mental health. Too much screen time, especially on social media, can cause anxiety, depression and low self-esteem, as people often compare themselves to idealised versions of others. The pressure to always be available adds stress and makes it hard to maintain a work-life balance. Digital platforms can also disrupt sleep and worsen mental health.

While digital tools have benefits, they also bring challenges. Many people, especially older generations, struggle to disconnect from the constant stream of emails and notifications, leading to stress and fatigue. Confusing software can cause frustration and hurt productivity. Younger generations may adapt more quickly, but older individuals may feel overwhelmed and have poor time management due to a steep learning curve. This constant connectivity makes it hard to set boundaries, as the pressure to stay connected can be overwhelming.

To protect your mental wellbeing, set clear boundaries for digital use, such as limiting screen time, avoiding emails after work, curating positive social media content and focusing on offline interactions. Organisations can help by using human-centred AI to create easy-to-use tools that reduce frustration and improve time management. Offering training for all age groups ensures everyone can benefit from technology without feeling overwhelmed.

Impacts on personal and professional relationships

Technology has dramatically impacted personal and professional relationships, changing how we connect and work. Remote work is a key example, showing how technology affects daily interactions. In *The Anxious Generation*, Jonathan Haidt highlights the adverse effects of smartphones (introduced in 2008) on work habits, puberty and rising anxiety levels.[116] He notes that changes in child-rearing practices also affect how young people face challenges. For those born *after* 1996, technology has shaped how they learn and build relationships. Parents and those born *before* 1996 may see these changes impact their parenting styles and their children's growth.

Working from home offers flexibility in male-dominated fields like STEM, helping women balance personal and professional duties. However, it also blurs the line between work and personal life, making it harder to disconnect, which can lead to stress and burnout. Women often feel extra pressure to prove themselves, leading to overwork and constant availability. This can be exhausting as they try to meet elevated expectations while juggling other responsibilities.

In personal relationships, technology has the capacity to help and to hurt. It allows us to stay connected with loved ones, despite distance, but can be a distraction that reduces quality time with family and friends. Women may be physically present but mentally occupied with work, which can strain relationships as loved ones may feel neglected. It is vital to set boundaries for technology use. That means setting aside time for personal interactions and disconnecting from work.

My strategy is not to have work emails on personal devices, like my phone, to prevent me from checking emails outside work hours. I also have a designated office at home. When I finish work for the day, I go through the important ritual of shutting down my computer, switching off the light and closing the door. Doing so protects my mental health, reduces stress and improves my relationships as I disconnect at the end of the day.

Creating healthy digital habits

Effective strategies can help address the challenges of digital device use, ensuring it supports rather than harms our wellbeing. The following practical steps will help you manage screen time, protect privacy and encourage healthier online interactions. Your goal is a more mindful and balanced use of technology.

Set screen time limits

Use tools like Screen Time on iOS or Digital Wellbeing on Android to track and limit your usage. Set daily limits for specific apps and aim for weekly or monthly screen time goals to stay mindful of your time spent on devices.

Take regular breaks from screens by using the Pomodoro Technique. I was introduced to this technique when I was studying at university. It involves working in 25-minute focused sessions, followed by 5-minute breaks. After four sessions, take a longer 15-30-minute break. This method helps maintain productivity, prevents screen fatigue and promotes a healthy balance with your digital habits. If you are like me and tend to ignore screen time limits, a good strategy is to connect with colleagues. Schedule short catchups, 15-25 minutes, to discuss topics or call a colleague while walking around. These provide breaks from technology to stretch your legs and stay connected with others.

Create tech-free zones and times

Create tech-free zones in your home, like your bedroom, to improve relaxation and sleep quality. Avoid blue light from phones and stop notifications from disturbing your rest. While challenging, setting tech-free times, such as during meals or an hour before bed, helps you unwind, reduces digital fatigue and strengthens relationships as you reconnect with loved ones. These moments allow for deeper connections and meaningful conversations. As Jonathan Haidt noted, tech-free periods also improve emotional intelligence and resilience.

Practice mindful usage

Be purposeful with your online activities. Set goals, like using social media for networking or learning instead of mindless scrolling. This mindful approach saves time and enriches your life. Regularly reflect on your online habits and adjust them to align with your values and wellbeing. By doing so, you can eliminate unhealthy patterns, reclaim time and focus on what truly matters, improving your quality of life.

Another way to be mindful is to delete social media apps from your phone and only use them on personal computers or through a web browser. I found constant notifications on my apps distracting as they encouraged me to scroll rather than concentrate on what I should be doing.

Establish boundaries for online interactions

Share your availability and response times with colleagues and clients to manage expectations and reduce the pressure to reply instantly. This supports a healthier work-life balance. Set specific times for checking emails and messages instead of staying constantly connected. This structure helps you focus better, lowers stress and keeps your personal time uninterrupted and more enjoyable.

Encourage offline activities

Engage in screen-free hobbies like reading, exercising or spending time outdoors. These activities help you disconnect from digital distractions, reduce eye strain and relax mentally, allowing you to enjoy the moment and boost your wellbeing.

Plan regular social events with friends and family to encourage face-to-face interactions. Reconnecting in person strengthens relationships and creates lasting memories. At least once a fortnight, I plan activities with family and friends to meet at a coffee shop, go to an event or meet at a park to go for a walk and chat. While it might sound simple, deliberately planning these activities and having others to do them with makes it more likely that I will get out and disconnect from technology.

Digital detox

Participate in digital detox challenges to promote balanced technology use. These activities offer a structured way to reduce screen time, helping you and your loved ones reconnect with the offline world and enjoy a healthier, less tech-dependent lifestyle.

Pushing back online and in-person

Managing your workload online and in person is essential in today's fast-paced, digital world. Women in STEM face extra challenges, so the following statements offer practical strategies to communicate boundaries, manage expectations and focus on what matters to prevent burnout.

> *** 'I appreciate the opportunity, but I currently have a full workload, so I cannot take on additional tasks at this time.'

> *** 'I am committed to delivering high-quality work, and adding more to my current workload would affect that standard. I hope you understand.'

> *** 'I am fully committed to my current responsibilities and won't be able to give additional tasks the attention they deserve. Can you find a solution that ensures everything gets done efficiently?'

> ** 'Thank you for considering me for this project. Unfortunately, my schedule is already packed, and I want to

ensure I can give my best effort to my current commitments.'

** *'I am currently focused on meeting several deadlines and can't take on more work without compromising quality. Perhaps we can discuss this after my current projects are completed.'*

** *'I understand the importance of this task, but I'm already at capacity. Is there someone else who could assist?'*

* *'I would love to help, but my plate is quite full right now. Can we revisit this in a few weeks?'*

* *'My schedule is quite tight at the moment, and I don't want to overextend myself. What would you like me to prioritise to achieve the most pressing item first?'*

These statements may seem simple, but they can be hard to say to your colleagues. Try practising in front of a mirror or saying them aloud as you get ready for work. Imagine speaking to those who push your boundaries. As you get more comfortable, using these techniques will feel less intimidating when the time comes. You can also communicate these messages through email when you receive a request electronically.

Intentional Networking

*I have learned that you can't have everything
and do everything at the same time.*
— OPRAH WINFREY [117]

Successful networking is about balancing meaningful connections without overextending yourself. Prioritise quality over quantity and focus on genuine relationships that offer mutual value and support. By setting clear goals and choosing the right opportunities, you can maintain your energy and build a supportive, lasting professional network rather than just collecting contacts.

The Boundary Blueprint

Building a strong professional network

The Covid pandemic expanded networking through technology and social media, allowing new opportunities and experiences. Networking events, in-person or online, feature different personalities, so knowing why you are networking and setting boundaries is essential.

Many of my close friendships started at networking events. However, if you are like me and shy away from networking due to its transactional feel, I recommend *Networking for People Who Hate Networking* by Devora Zack.[118] It is great for introverts, focusing on authentic connections rather than superficial ones.

Chapter 12: Intentional Networking

Zack (also an introvert) shares practical advice for using your natural strengths, like listening and building deep relationships, to redefine networking in a way that feels comfortable to you.

If you want to build a meaningful professional network without compromising your boundaries, you must understand the difference between transactional and transformational networking styles. The difference will maintain boundaries and make lasting connections that support your goals.

Transactional networking

Transactional networking focuses on quick value exchange, making interactions impersonal and one-sided. Its lack of depth can drain your energy, leaving the experience superficial and unfulfilling. The constant need to switch gears and engage in shallow interactions can be mentally and emotionally exhausting, leading to burnout and a sense of wasted time.

One typical example is the rapid exchange of business cards or LinkedIn connection details with minimal conversation, resulting in a collection of contacts but no substantial connections. This repetitive process feels insincere and unproductive, reducing the overall value of the networking experience. I have become adept at spotting people who use this approach by observing the body language of everyone in the room. People who engage in this type of networking often seem disengaged, and their body language reveals they are there for personal gain.

Another form of transactional networking is the constant delivery of sales pitches, where individuals push their products without mutual interest. Some people focus solely on job hunting or gathering information, offering nothing in return, which can feel exploitative and draining. Event hopping, where people move from one person to another without forming meaningful connections, also makes networking feel like a checklist rather than an opportunity for natural growth.

A PERSONAL PERSPECTIVE

I encountered a classic example of transactional networking at a recent professional networking event. Early in the evening, a man approached me with a confident smile. After introducing himself, he quickly launched into an extensive monologue about his impressive achievements, focusing on his skills, projects and the high-profile clients he had worked with. Throughout our interaction, he scarcely paused to ask questions about me or my interests; he was only interested in my job role and who I knew.

His primary focus was clearly on understanding whether I could be a valuable contact or how he could leverage my connections for his benefit. That became apparent as he probed about the people I knew and how they might align with his business goals. His lack of genuine engagement and disregard for personal connection made it easy to spot the transactional nature of his approach.

The encounter was unfulfilling and a stark reminder of how transactional networking can feel impersonal and self-serving. It highlighted the importance of genuine, transformational networking, where building meaningful relationships takes precedence over immediate gains.

Chapter 12: Intentional Networking

Transformational networking

Lasting professional relationships are more important than ever in our world of instant, yet often distant, connections.

Transformational networking focuses on genuine connections that lead to personal and professional growth. Unlike transactional networking, which is based on quick value exchanges, transformational networking builds deep relationships founded on trust, shared values and a genuine interest in each other's success. These connections go beyond exchanging business cards — they create support systems that inspire collaboration and innovation. By prioritising transformational relationships, individuals build lasting, meaningful partnerships that benefit their careers and contribute to a more robust professional community.

> Prioritise forming genuine relationships over quick wins.

For more on this, I recommend reading *The Long Game: How to Be a Long-Term Thinker in a Short-Term World* by Dorie Clark.[119] When it comes to networking, Clark emphasises that we should prioritise forming genuine relationships over quick wins. She encourages investing time in understanding and supporting others rather than seeking immediate benefits. We foster trust and reliability by focusing on authentic, mutually beneficial connections and long-term value. Clark also stresses the importance of consistency and follow-up to keep these relationships strong and supportive over time.

I apply these principles in simple ways, like tagging someone in a LinkedIn story that reminds me of them, sending a heartfelt birthday message or just checking in. It feels great when someone does this for me. A memorable moment for me was when an old acquaintance reached out privately on LinkedIn to thank me for advice I had given him years before that had changed his life. I had not realised how impactful our brief conversation was until then.

Why not try it? You never know who you may be helping in the long run by simply being humble and kind. A small act of kindness can make a massive impact.

At a recent workshop, I coached a group of professionals on adopting a more transformational networking approach. Networking is not a transaction. It should focus on building genuine connections, not resemble a speed dating event.

Here are three practical tips I shared.

Start conversations with open-ended questions, such as, 'What brings you here?' rather than immediately introducing themselves with their company and credentials. This approach encourages others to share their stories and experiences, creating a more engaging dialogue.

Remember the importance of giving heartfelt compliments that go beyond physical appearance. For instance, complimenting someone on a unique piece of jewellery or a well-chosen accessory like a tie can create a positive atmosphere. We feel validated and connected when our taste is recognised and praised.

Lead with inspiring questions that foster deeper conversations like 'What are you passionate about in your work?' or 'What exciting activities are you currently involved in?' These questions uncover shared interests and values, laying the groundwork for a lasting connection. The goal of transformational networking is about genuine interest in others, mutual support and building relationships that offer long-term benefits.

Don't step on their toes

Improving your networking style while respecting others' boundaries and protecting your own is essential for building authentic and lasting professional relationships. I recommend two great books that will assist you in being authentic to your values and beliefs.

Awaken Your Genius by Ozan Varol is a guide to unlocking creativity and thinking differently for success.[120] To build genuine relationships based on respect and shared ideas, Varol says to stay true to your ideas and values instead of conforming or saying what others want to hear. He also stresses the importance of clear boundaries, ensuring your individuality is not compromised. You form meaningful, lasting connections by being true to yourself and respecting others' boundaries.

The Art of Possibility by Rosamund Stone Zander and Benjamin Zander.[121] This book focuses on genuine connections and mutual contributions and promotes curiosity and openness that lead to respectful and enriching interactions. The Zanders encourage us to put ourselves in the other person's shoes and recognise contributions without dominating the conversation. Stay curious about others' values and beliefs, even if they differ from yours, and use the opportunity to learn. This approach helps develop authentic networking practices while staying true to your values and boundaries. Networking becomes less daunting when you take it as an opportunity to learn and grow. It's more about forming meaningful connections rather than superficial exchanges.

The Zanders highlight the power of contribution in building meaningful relationships, which benefits you overall. In networking, that means focusing on giving rather than taking. By helping others succeed, you create more robust, authentic connections. This approach supports personal boundaries by fostering respectful, mutually beneficial relationships that make networking more enriching and less transactional.

The balancing act

Balancing networking with other commitments can be particularly challenging for women working in STEM with family or other responsibilities.

As a single mother for a significant part of my life, especially after leaving the military, I knew I needed to build new networks. But I did not want to be defined by labels like 'veteran' or 'single mother'. While we do not like stereotyping, labels are shortcuts that can make us feel comfortable. Sometimes, I would talk about my military career to cover insecurities or to show I had something in common with whoever I was talking to. The problem is that we sometimes avoid stretching ourselves and tend to gravitate towards people more like ourselves. Or we can use our 'other commitments' as reasons to avoid attending new or different networking events.

To manage this balance, I recommend carefully selecting suitable events to attend. Focus on the purpose behind your attendance and set clear objectives. Women with additional commitments should prioritise these to make their networking efforts more meaningful and impactful.

Choose the right event

When balancing networking with other commitments, prioritise quality over quantity. Instead of attending many events, focus on those offering the most value. For example, attend conferences related to the field you want to break into or workshops where you can meet key industry players and gain specific knowledge and skills relevant to your goals. I once advised a client to attend a niche technical conference instead of several general networking mixers, which resulted in her forming valuable connections and learning about innovative research in her field.

Leverage virtual events

Virtual networking lets you connect with others from home, making it easier to balance family commitments. I often join webinars and online forums for coaching and mentoring, which helps expand my network without the need for travel. Virtual events also allow you to meet people with shared interests and broaden your areas of interest and circle of influence. All without leaving home.

Be selective about your attendance

If you attend an event in person, pick those that fit your schedule and do not clash with family duties. Evening or weekend events might work better if you are busy during the day. I once suggested a Saturday morning networking brunch to a client with young children. This better suited her schedule as she got her partner to watch the kids. The meetup led to valuable collaborations in a relaxed atmosphere.

Join STEM professional associations and meetups

These groups often provide virtual and in-person options, making it easier to choose what suits you. For example, a client joined a women-in-tech group and attended monthly virtual meetups. She built a supportive network while managing her family duties, growing personally and professionally without compromising her other commitments.

Know why you're attending

When networking, it is essential to define your goals. Know what you want to achieve from an event. Is it finding mentors, learning new trends or seeking collaboration? One of my clients attended a conference to find a mentor in AI research. With this focus, she was able to make meaningful connections with industry leaders.

Chapter 12: Intentional Networking

Preparation can make all the difference. Identify the key people you would like to connect with and know why you want to do so. At conferences, do you want to meet attendees or speakers? I advised a client to do this for a Women in STEMM (includes medicine) leadership symposium. She found people working on similar projects, which led to engaging conversations.

Plan your schedule to get the most out of the event. Arrive early, attend key sessions and be strategic about who you spend time with. Remember the difference between transactional and transformational networking. Once you spot the transactional networkers, politely excuse yourself and focus on more meaningful connections. Here are some phrases you can use to exit those conversations politely.

'It's been great chatting with you, but I must catch up with a colleague before the next session.'

'Thank you for sharing about your work. I promised to meet with a few more people tonight, so perhaps we can catch up later.'

'I appreciate the information. I will take a moment to grab a drink, but it was nice meeting you.'

'I enjoyed our conversation. I'm here to meet a few specific people tonight, so I must move on. Let's connect on LinkedIn.'

'It was nice learning about your projects. I need to speak with a couple of other folks before the event ends. Have a great evening!'

After the event, follow up with new contacts meaningfully and personally. Mention something specific they said or what you liked about them. A brief email or message helps strengthen the connection for future interactions. For example, one of my clients followed my suggestion to attend a virtual STEM meetup. Afterwards, she connected with several key contacts on LinkedIn, transforming the initial interaction into a lasting relationship.

I also believe in paying it forward by introducing others who might benefit from the connection. It not only feels good but helps you stay memorable. As the saying goes, 'It's not what you know, but who you know,' which is critical to building lasting relationships.

Chapter 12: Intentional Networking

Balancing networking with family commitments

Before I left the military, people often asked how I managed everything — working full-time, studying part-time and being a single parent. It was not about perfect time management but prioritising what mattered most to me at the time. There is really no such thing as an ideal work-life balance, especially with young children and competing priorities.

When I decided to leave the military, I spent three years planning my discharge date, focusing on preparing for a civilian career, providing stability for my daughters, settling into a new house and building new networks. It was challenging, but I always had a plan and a backup plan.

Have a plan

Many people face challenges in pursuing their important goals due to family commitments or time constraints, often because they lack a clear plan or do not have backup options. Tasks invariably take longer than expected, and leaving things to the last minute causes unnecessary stress. Setting boundaries and priorities protects your wellbeing while meeting your commitments. Successfully balancing new networking opportunities with family responsibilities requires recognising their importance and making them a priority.

Manage your time

Effective time management and knowing your priorities are essential when balancing networking and family. Whenever I coach a new client, I have them do a Wheel of Life assessment to evaluate different areas of their life and identify what is working well and what is not. Then, I ask them to track their daily activities for a week. This process often reveals overlooked timewasters that need attention to pursue new goals and growth.

For an example and instructions on conducting a Wheel of Life, refer to Appendix 7.

Strengthen boundaries

Knowing where to improve and strengthen your boundaries makes you feel more grounded and less stressed. Identifying timewasters is the first step to achieving better balance, especially during busy times or emergencies. Use time management tools to organise your schedule, allowing specific times for networking, family and social commitments so nothing gets overlooked.

Share your schedule with your family and stick to it, being firm but kind when communicating your boundaries. For example, a client informed her family about her networking events in advance, enabling her to attend without guilt or interruptions.

Master the juggle

As someone who is always on the go but has a not-so-great memory, I have developed a habit of emailing myself to-do lists or updating my digital calendar whenever inspiration hits, even at odd times.

If someone asks me to do something, I ask them to email me with the details. That achieves two things: it prompts them to follow up, showing the task is important to them, and it helps me avoid overcommitting to things that might not be as important to me. That way, I ensure time for essential activities and manage my schedule more effectively. People often comment on how much I fit into my day. It's only possible because I intentionally align my commitments with my values, priorities and goals.

Use support networks

Use your support network. Involving your spouse, partner, friends or family to help with family duties makes a significant difference.

If you don't have a built-in support network, get creative and reach out for help. Calling in hired help, as I did when I needed a babysitter to attend work functions, can be a lifesaver. Services like professional babysitters or even on-demand childcare can give you the flexibility you need. There's peace of mind with these services as they have working with children checks and you get to interview them, just as you would a prospective employee. If hiring help isn't feasible, consider asking a neighbour, a coworker or a casual acquaintance you trust. Many people are happy to lend a hand when approached with honesty and gratitude.

For example, one client without close family nearby started a babysitting swap with a neighbour. She offered to watch their children when needed, and in return, they supported her during critical work events. This arrangement eased her immediate childcare needs and helped build a supportive relationship within her community. Such small, intentional efforts can create a network of support over time, even if it doesn't seem readily available at first.

Remember, seeking support isn't a sign of weakness; it's a strategic way to prioritise your goals while maintaining balance.

Take care of yourself

Balancing networking and family can be demanding, so prioritising self-care helps prevent burnout. I make sure to schedule regular downtime for activities like reading or exercising. When I shared this with a client, she started taking daily walks, which helped her stay refreshed and energised. Prioritising self-care boosts your resilience and allows you to confidently meet your commitments.

While taking a break when you are under pressure may seem counterintuitive, stepping back for a short walk or stretch can help reset your priorities and objectives. I always remind myself that someone else's poor planning or prioritisation is not necessarily my problem. Making it your problem leads to boundary violations, signalling that your time is less valuable. That is not where you want to be.

Chapter 12: Intentional Networking

 Guiding questions

To wrap up this chapter, evaluate how you set boundaries when networking is vital to fostering confidence and preventing burnout. Knowing and respecting your limits helps create a healthier work-life balance, increasing satisfaction and productivity. It is important to remember that navigating networking opportunities and building connections without compromising your values, time and other commitments can be challenging. Consider these questions to help you maintain a balanced and practical approach:

1. What are my core values and priorities in my personal and professional life? How do these influence the boundaries I set when networking and building connections?

2. What boundaries do I currently have in place for networking? Are they effective in maintaining a healthy balance between my personal and professional commitments?

3. Am I comfortable communicating my boundaries to new contacts and colleagues? What strategies can I use to improve this communication during networking events?

4. Do I feel overwhelmed by my networking commitments? How can I delegate tasks or decline additional networking activities in a way that aligns with my boundaries?

5. Am I dedicating too much time to networking beyond my designated hours? How can I better manage my time to avoid overextending myself?

6. Do I make enough time for myself and my personal life amidst networking? What activities or time slots can I reserve strictly for personal use to recharge?

7. How can I involve my support network (for example, family, friends, colleagues) to help manage my responsibilities and uphold my networking boundaries?

8. Am I prioritising self-care and wellbeing while networking? What changes can I make to ensure I am taking care of myself?

9. What have I learned from past experiences about setting and maintaining boundaries in professional settings? How can I apply these lessons to improve my current approach?

10. How do my networking activities affect my long-term career goals and personal happiness? Are there any adjustments I need to make to align them better with my future aspirations?

And Finally ...

You've probably realised by now that I am fanatical about boundaries for women, especially those in STEM and male-dominated workplaces. That's why I wrote this book. Throughout these pages, I have explored the challenges of setting and defending personal and professional boundaries, especially in the context of gender dynamics and societal expectations.

Setting boundaries isn't just about defining limits; it's about developing the resilience to uphold them, even when faced with pressure. Resilience is key to protecting your wellbeing and staying firm in your decisions.

Many of us struggle with managing intellectual, emotional and physical boundaries. When not properly enforced, these boundaries can lead to unhealthy dynamics, triggering strong emotional and physical reactions. Understanding these responses is essential to protecting yourself, so I've provided tools and strategies to help you manage these challenges effectively.

Societal pressures, especially on women, make boundary-setting more difficult. Media, culture and religious expectations often undermine our ability to assert ourselves. Gender bias, particularly in male-dominated fields like STEM, further weakens boundaries. Inclusivity is vital, and I've shared how male colleagues and leaders can support women in maintaining healthy boundaries.

Workplace dynamics complicate boundary-setting. Overstepping boundaries can create guilt and fear, but using the strategies discussed in this book can confidently strengthen your professional boundaries and navigate these situations. Additionally, managing the boundaries of others — often challenged by resistance, stereotypes or disrespect — requires effort and self-awareness.

Balancing career and personal life is a challenge many women face, particularly in fast-paced industries. I've offered strategies to align personal values with professional goals, avoid burnout and maintain a healthy work-life balance. With these tools, you will create lasting, positive change in your life and relationships.

Three steps to success

To summarise everything you've read in this book, here is a simple three-step (triple S) technique to effectively manage and adapt your boundaries.

Self-reflection — Regularly assess your boundaries and how they align with your life goals and circumstances. Reflect on what is working and what needs adjustment.

Seek feedback — Ask trusted colleagues, mentors and friends for their perspectives on your boundaries. They can offer insights you might not have considered.

Set clear goals — Define what you need to protect and why, to establish and maintain the boundaries that support your wellbeing and success.

If you feel that your boundaries have been compromised, it's important to acknowledge that setbacks are a natural part of life. They don't define you, but how you respond to them can

And Finally ...

shape your future. Whether you have a personal or professional challenge, the key to moving forward is rebuilding and reaffirming your boundaries.

Rebuilding after a setback

Setbacks are part of life. Here are some strategies to rebuild your boundaries after life hits a glitch.

Self-compassion — Treat yourself with kindness and understanding. Acknowledge that setbacks are growth opportunities.

Reflect on the setback — Understand what led to the boundary violation and what you can learn from it. Use this knowledge to strengthen your boundaries.

Future self letter — Write a letter to your future self. Outline the lessons learned and the boundaries you need to protect moving forward. This exercise can reinforce your commitment to maintaining strong boundaries.

Rebuilding after a setback is not a one-time exercise; it's an ongoing process. As you restore your boundaries, remember to keep them flexible and adaptable, allowing for growth and change. The work doesn't stop once you've regained your footing.

Renew, review, change, repeat

Keep things simple — the easier they are, the more manageable life becomes. Effective boundaries require a continuous cycle of renewal, review and change. Here is how to apply this cycle:

Renewal — Regularly recharge your commitment to your boundaries. Remind yourself why they are important and how they benefit you.

Review — Examine your boundaries periodically to ensure they are still relevant and effective. Adjust them as needed based on your current circumstances.

Change — Do not be afraid to make changes. Adaptability is crucial in maintaining boundaries that serve your evolving needs.

The key is to do it regularly — whenever you experience a significant life change, at least once a year, or when you feel stuck or burnt out. When coaching clients who feel stuck, I have them write a letter to their future selves, focusing on the goals they want to achieve and the boundaries holding them back. They reflect on how far they have come and the challenges they have faced. I use this technique because my first coach did the same for me, and it helped me overcome limiting beliefs. Try it — it might work for you too!

Let me help you

My goal in this book was to offer practical tools, insights and encouragement to help you navigate boundary challenges while maintaining your personal and professional integrity. However, setting and keeping boundaries often needs ongoing support and tailored guidance; that is where I can help you further.

Individual coaching

Personalised coaching sessions can help you dive deeper into your unique boundary issues, offering targeted strategies to address specific challenges in your life. Whether you struggle to set limits at work, find balance in personal relationships or manage your time and energy effectively, one-on-one coaching provides a confidential space to explore your concerns and develop practical solutions. Together, we work on recognising where your boundaries are being compromised, identifying areas of improvement and implementing action plans so you can stand firm.

Workshops and group sessions

I also offer workshops to tackle common boundary issues in professional and personal contexts. These interactive sessions provide a collaborative environment where you can learn from others facing similar challenges, share experiences and build confidence in asserting your needs. The workshops cover topics like setting healthy boundaries with colleagues, managing work-life balance and developing resilience against boundary violations. You will leave equipped with actionable strategies, tools and a community of support to reinforce your journey.

Resources and tools

Beyond coaching and workshops, I have a wealth of resources you can access at your own pace. These include downloadable guides, boundary-setting worksheets, self-assessment tools and recommended readings that deepen your understanding of maintaining strong boundaries. I continually update these resources to ensure they remain relevant and valuable as you progress. Email me julia@winterandassociates.com.au for your free resource kit on setting and maintaining boundaries.

If you're ready to take the next step in mastering your boundaries, I invite you to explore the available coaching options, workshops and resources at www.winterandassociates.com.au. Whether you need direct support or simply want to access additional materials referenced in this book, you will find everything you need to empower yourself to create the balanced, respectful life you deserve.

Appendix 1

Values Identification Exercise

This exercise explores what matters most to you by combining a multiple-choice activity and value lists. It is designed to clarify your core values, offering insights into how they shape your boundaries, decisions and relationships. There are no right or wrong answers, just what feels most like you.

Step 1: Reflective questions

Answer the following questions by selecting the option that resonates most with you:

1. **When faced with a difficult decision, what do you prioritise?**
    a) honesty and integrity
    b) success and achievement
    c) connection and belonging
    d) fairness and equality
    e) growth and learning.

2. **What motivates you most in your personal and professional life?**

    a) helping others
    b) being recognised for your accomplishments
    c) developing meaningful relationships
    d) solving problems and finding innovative solutions
    e) living with purpose and authenticity.

3. **Which statement best reflects your view of success?**

    a) building a life of balance and harmony
    b) achieving significant milestones
    c) making a positive impact on others
    d) continuously learning and improving
    e) standing up for your beliefs and making a difference.

4. **Which of the following environments or situations do you feel most comfortable in?**

    a) a fast-paced, high-energy setting where I can take on multiple tasks at once
    b) a calm, peaceful space with minimal distractions where I can focus deeply
    c) a collaborative, team-oriented atmosphere where ideas are shared and discussed
    d) a competitive, goal-driven environment where I can measure my achievements
    e) a supportive, nurturing space where relationships and emotional connections are prioritised.

Appendix 1: Values Identification Exercise

Step 2: Values list

Review the following values and circle or highlight five that best reflect what matters to you.

Achievement	Adventure	Authenticity
Balance	Compassion	Creativity
Fairness	Family	Freedom
Growth	Honesty	Integrity
Justice	Kindness	Learning
Loyalty	Perseverance	Respect
Security	Spirituality	Trustworthiness

Step 3: Narrow down your top values

From your selected values, narrow the list to your top three values. These should reflect the principles that guide your behaviour and decisions, even in challenging situations.

Step 4: Reflective prompts

Use these prompts to gain deeper insight into how your values influence your boundaries:

How do these values show up in your daily life?

Have there been moments when you compromised one of these values? How did it feel?

What boundaries can you set to protect and honour these values?

Appendix 2

Parenting Programs and Resource Guide

Raising Children Network (RCN)

https://raisingchildren.net.au/

This website is for Australian parents, grandparents or anyone responsible for the care of children. RCN is a source of information for parents. The website includes various professionals and agencies who work with parents, such as general practitioners, maternal and child health nurses, childcare workers, preschool teachers, school teachers, social workers and psychologists.

Parentline

https://services.dffh.vic.gov.au/parentline

A confidential telephone counselling service providing professional counselling and support for parents and those who care for children. Parentline aims to nurture and support positive, caring relationships between parents, children, teenagers and significant other people who are important to the wellbeing of families.

Appendix 2: Parenting Programs and Resource Guide

Family Services Australia

https://familyservices.org.au/thoughtful-parenting/

Provides services promoting change and opportunities for children, young people and families to build on their relationships and connect with their communities. They have a special emphasis on building and strengthening parenting skills.

Karitane

https://karitane.com.au/

A pioneering not-for-profit organisation and registered charity offering expert parental support, education and advice to help families navigate the first 2000 days of their child's life.

World Organization for Humanitarian Movement (WOHM)

https://wohum.org/about-us/

A global organisation that empowers parents globally to raise resilient, responsible and compassionate children who reach their full potential.

ACT Raising Safe Kids Program

https://www.apa.org/act

This program from the American Psychological Association has a wealth of information in downloadable factsheets and handouts for parents and caregivers.

Appendix 3

Domestic and Family Violence Support Services

If you or someone you know is experiencing domestic violence in Australia, there are many excellent resources available for support and information:

1-800-RESPECT

Phone: 1800 737 732 (1800RESPECT)

National counselling service violence, providing 24/7 confidential support for victims of sexual assault, domestic and family.

Lifeline

Phone: 13 11 14

National crisis support service offering 24/7 phone and online counselling for those needing immediate assistance.

https://toolkit.lifeline.org.au/topics/domestic-and-family-violence/support-services-for-domestic-and-family-violence

Appendix 3: Domestic and Family Violence Support Services

Full Stop Australia

Phone: 1800 385 578

Free, confidential, 24/7 counselling service for anyone impacted by domestic and family violence.

Kids Helpline

Phone: 1800 551 800

Free, confidential, 24/7 service for kids, teens, young people and adults who care about them.

MensLine Australia

Phone: 1300 789 978

Free, confidential, 24/7 counselling, information and referral service for men with mental health, anger management, relationship, family violence, addiction and wellbeing concerns.

Men's Referral Service

Phone: 1300 766 491

Free, confidential, 24/7 counselling, information and referral service for men using violence and abuse in their relationships.

Reachout

https://au.reachout.com/challenges-and-coping/abuse-and-violence

Offers anonymous, confidential support, helping young people express themselves, gain perspective, connect without judgment and build resilience for life's challenges.

White Ribbon Australia

https://whiteribbon.org.au/helplines/

Works to end men's violence against women through advocacy, education and cultural change for a safer society.

Appendix 4

Recommended Readings

(on Communication Styles and Supportive Environments for Neurodivergent Individuals)

Armstrong, T. *(2011). The Power of Neurodiversity: Unleashing the advantages of your differently wired brain.* Da Capo Lifelong Books.

Discusses how neurodivergent individuals can be supported in various settings, especially in the workplace, emphasising strengths rather than weaknesses.

Baron-Cohen, S. *(2012). The Essential Difference: Men, women and the extreme male brain.* Penguin Press.

Explores gender differences in communication styles, emphasising how neurodivergent individuals may need tailored supportive environments to thrive.

Dunne, M. *(2024). The Neurodiversity Edge: The essential guide to embracing autism, ADHD, dyslexia, and other neurological differences for any organization.* John Wiley & Sons.

An essential guide for executives, board directors, human resources professionals, managers, recruiters, entrepreneurs, venture capitalists, allies, educators, nonprofit leaders and anyone with an interest in better understanding neurodiversity, authentic neuroinclusion and the human mind.

Grandin, T. *(2020). Different...Not Less: Inspiring stories of achievement and successful employment from adults with autism, Asperger's and ADHD (Revised and Updated).* Future Horizons.

Temple Grandin's autobiographical work of fourteen unique individuals illustrates the extraordinary potential of those on the autism spectrum and shows how to work with them.

HoneyBourne, V. *(2019). The Neurodiverse Workplace: An employer's guide to managing and working with neurodivergent employees, clients and customers.* Jessica Kingsley Publishers.

This practical, authoritative business guide helps managers and employers support neurodiverse staff and gives advice on how to ensure workplaces are neuro-friendly.

Nerenberg, J. *(2021). Divergent Mind: Thriving in a world that wasn't designed for you.* HarperCollins.

Nerenberg examines how neurodivergent individuals, particularly women, experience unique communication styles and require specific supportive environments to thrive, highlighting strategies for success.

Appendix 4: Recommended Readings

Praslova, L. *(2024). The Canary Code: A guide to neurodiversity, dignity and intersectional belonging at work.* Berrett-Koehler Publishers.

A groundbreaking framework for intersectional inclusion and belonging at work that embraces human cognitive, emotional and neurobiological differences — neurodiversity.

Appendix 5

Extra Resources to Learn Assertiveness Skills

The following list includes resources for learning assertiveness skills to communicate boundaries effectively:

Books

Assertiveness: How to stand up for yourself and still win the respect of others by Judy Murphy.

The Assertiveness Workbook: How to express your ideas and stand up for yourself at work and in relationships by Randy J. Paterson.

Stop People Pleasing: Be assertive, stop caring what others think, beat your guilt, & stop being a pushover by Patrick King.

Setting Boundaries: Care for yourself and stop being controlled by others by Dr Rebecca Ray.

Set Boundaries, Find Peace: A guide to reclaiming yourself by Nedra Glover Tawwab.

Appendix 5: Extra Resources to Learn Assertiveness Skills

Boundaries: Where You End and I Begin: How to Recognise and Set Healthy Boundaries by Anne Katherine.

Daring Greatly: How the courage to be vulnerable transforms the way we live, love, parent and lead by Brené Brown.

Shame and Guilt by June Price Tangney and Ronda L. Dearing.

Workshops and seminars

Look for local workshops or seminars on assertiveness training and effective communication skills.

Many counselling centres and community organisations offer workshops on assertiveness and boundary setting.

Online Courses

Udemy https://www.udemy.com/ offers courses on assertiveness training and effective communication.

Coursera https://www.coursera.org/ provides courses on communication skills and assertiveness training.

LinkedIn Learning https://www.linkedin.com/learning/ offers a variety of courses on assertiveness and boundary setting.

Therapy or counselling

Consider seeking therapy or counselling from a licensed therapist specialising in assertiveness training and communication skills.

Individual therapy sessions can provide personalised guidance and support in learning assertiveness skills.

Practice exercises

Practice assertiveness through role-playing exercises with a friend, family member or coach.

A good resource that has videos can be found at **Mindowl.org** *https://mindowl.org/examples-of-assertive-communication/*

Journaling can help reflect on past interactions and identify areas for improvement in assertive communication.

Online resources

For articles and resources on assertiveness training and effective communication techniques, go to:

Psychology Today *https://www.psychologytoday.com/au*

Verywell Mind *.https://www.verywellmind.com/*

YouTube channels and podcasts focused on personal development and communication skills may also provide valuable insights and tips.

Appendix 5: Extra Resources to Learn Assertiveness Skills

Assertiveness training groups

Look for assertiveness training groups or support groups in your community where you can learn from others and practice assertiveness skills in a supportive environment.

Remember that learning assertiveness takes time and practice, so be patient with yourself as you improve your communication and boundary-setting abilities.

Appendix 6

Self-Evaluation of Your Work-Life Balance

Goal setting

- What are your short- and long-term goals in your career and personal life?
- How do you identify and track these?
- How do these goals align with your core values and desired outcomes?
- How often do you review and adjust your goals to ensure they remain relevant?
- Where can you set specific goals for increasing collaboration within your current projects?
- How can you measure the success of these collaborative efforts?

Time management

- How do you track how you spend your time over a week or month?
- Which activities drain your energy versus those that invigorate you?

- How do you prioritise tasks that align with your values and goals?
- How accurately do you estimate the time required to complete tasks?
- Do you often underestimate or overestimate the time required, leading to unnecessary stress or wasted time?
- What portion of your day is dedicated to work versus personal activities?
- How can you reallocate your time to ensure you are not neglecting either area?

Boundary creation

- How well do you set and enforce boundaries between work and personal time?
- Do you check work emails or think about work during your personal time?
- How do you communicate your boundaries to your employers, colleagues and family members?
- What challenges do you face in maintaining these boundaries? How do you address them?
- How well do you communicate your work hours and availability to colleagues, clients and family members?
- Do you have clear boundaries? How often are they respected?
- What steps can you take to ensure you are not overcommitting to work or personal obligations, leading to burnout?

Flexibility and adaptability

- How do you typically respond to unexpected changes or challenges in your work or personal life?
- Are you generally adaptable, or do you struggle with rigidity and control?
- Can you recall a time when you had to adapt your plans due to shifting priorities? What happened? How did you overcome it?
- What strategies can you implement to become more flexible and open to change, allowing you to better navigate the uncertainties and demands of your professional and personal life?
- What strategies do you use to handle unexpected interruptions or changes to your schedule?
- How can you improve your flexibility without compromising your balance?

Support systems

- How often do you delegate tasks in your professional and personal life?
- Are you considered unhelpfully independent?
- What does it take for you to allow people to support you?
- When are you willing to accept help? Why?
- When are you not willing to accept help? Why not?
- Who are the key members of your support system? How do you utilise them?
- What prevents you from asking for help? How do you overcome this barrier?

Appendix 6: Self-Evaluation of Your Work-Life Balance

Self-care

- What changes can you make to your daily routine to enhance your overall wellbeing and satisfaction with your work and personal life?
- What activities do you engage in to promote your physical, mental and emotional health?
- How do you ensure that self-care remains a priority, even during busy times?
- What self-care practices do you have in place to recharge and prevent burnout?
- How can you ensure you regularly make time for these activities?
- How satisfied are you with your current work-life balance?
- What aspects of your life do you feel are lacking attention or causing stress?

Feedback and self-reflection

- How do you seek feedback on your strengths, weaknesses and areas for improvement?
- How do you differentiate between helpful feedback and feedback with hidden agendas?
- What role does self-reflection play in your personal and professional growth? How do you practice it?
- When do you schedule regular check-ins or feedback sessions with your colleagues or mentors?
- How can you create an open environment where team members feel comfortable sharing their ideas and suggestions?

Reassessing values

- How often do you reassess your values and priorities to ensure they align with your current goals?
- What triggers you to re-evaluate your values and make necessary adjustments?
- How do you track your progress in aligning your actions with your values over time?
- What core values are most important to you personally and professionally?
- How well do your current activities and commitments align with these values?
- Have any recent experiences or changes in your life shifted your values or priorities?
- How can you adjust your goals and actions to reflect these changes?

Mindfulness practices

- What mindfulness practices do you engage in to enhance self-awareness and decision-making clarity?
- How do these practices help you manage stress and maintain emotional regulation?
- How often do you take time for mindfulness practices, such as meditation, deep breathing or mindful walking?
- How do these practices impact your stress levels and overall wellbeing?
- Can you share an example of how mindfulness has positively impacted your work or personal life?
- How can you incorporate mindfulness into your daily routine to enhance your focus, reduce stress and improve your work-life balance?

Appendix 7

Wheel of Life

Directions: The eight sections in the wheel of life represent life balance. There are 10 circles representing scores from 0 (in the centre) to 10 on the outer circle. Rank your level of satisfaction with each area of your life by filling in where you are at.

This represents how balanced or unbalanced you view your life and the lower the circle area, the more room for improvement.

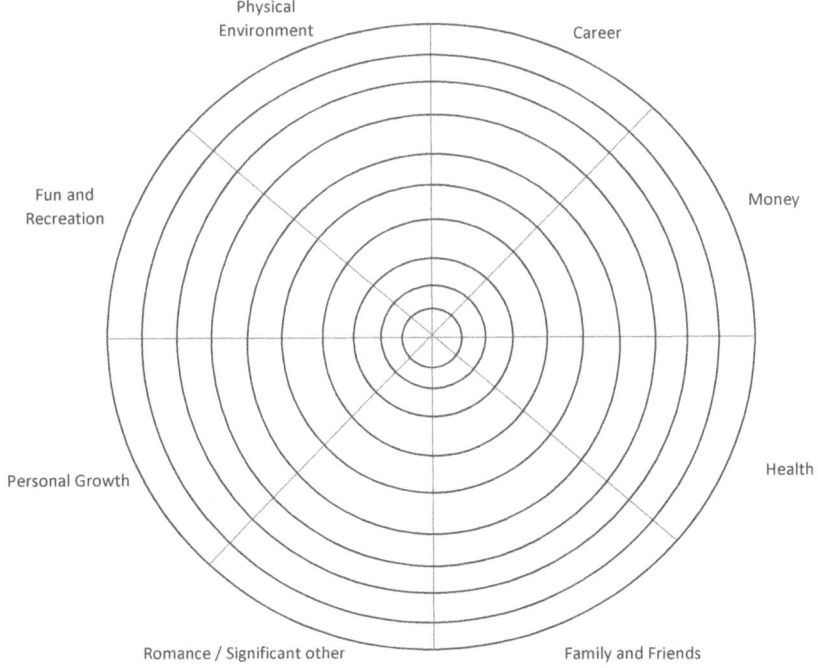

References

1. Parliamentary Workplace Support Service. (2024). *What is Neurodiversity*. Available at: https://www.pwss.gov.au/sites/default/files/Neurodiversity%20Fact%20Sheet.pdf.

2. Australian Public Service Commission. (2023). *Understanding neurodiversity in the APS*. Available at: https://www.apsc.gov.au/initiatives-and-programs/workforce-information/research-analysis-and-publications/state-service/state-service-report-2023/aps-profile/understanding-neurodiversity-aps.

3. Nix, K., Seals, C. and DeLoach, K. (2024). Neurodiverse Minds in STEM: A Literature Review Exploring the Link between Representation and School Adaptation. *IntechOpen eBooks*. doi:https://doi.org/10.5772/intechopen.1007854.

4. Australian Disability Network. (2024). *What is Neurodiversity*. Available at: https://australiandisabilitynetwork.org.au/wp-content/uploads/2024/11/What-is-neurodiversity.pdf.

5. Baron-Cohen, S. (2012). *The Essential Difference: Men, Women and the Extreme Male Brain*. Penguin Press.

6. Stanton, T. (2023). *Understanding Neurodiversity: How Many Neurodivergent People Are There?* [online] neurodiversity.guru. Available at: https://www.neurodiversity.guru/how-many-neurodivergent-are-there.

7. Brown, B. (2010). *The Gifts of Imperfection: Let Go of Who You Think You're Supposed to Be and Embrace Who You Are*. Center City, Minn.: Hazelden.

8. Collette, T. (nd). Available at: https://www.imdb.com/name/nm0001057/quotes/.

9. Eurich, T. (2017). *Insight: The surprising truth about how others see us and how we see ourselves, and why the answers matter more than we think*. Currency Books.

10. World Economic Forum (2021). *Global Gender Gap Report 2021*. [online] World Economic Forum. Available at: https://www3.weforum.org/docs/WEF_GGGR_2021.pdf.

11. Amen, D. (2024, March 25). *3 Steps to Stop your brain's guilt cycle and how to re-parent yourself to build mental strength*. PODCAST- On Purpose with Jay Shetty.

12. Shetty, J. (2024). *Jay Shetty and Dr Daniel Amen on 3 ways to stop your brains guilt cycle*, website. Available at: https://www.jayshetty.me/blog/jay-shetty-dr-daniel-amen-on-3-ways-to-stop-your-brains-guilt-cycle.

13. Smith, W. (2018, Jan 30). *Fault Vs Responsibility*. You Tube. Available at: Fault Vs Responsibility Will Smith EPIC MOTIVATION - YouTube.

14. American Psychological Association. (2013). *How stress affects your health*. Available at: https://www.apa.org/topics/stress/health.

15. American Psychological Association. (2018). *Stress effects on the body*. Available at: https://www.apa.org/topics/stress/body.

16. Gibney, J. (2023). *Break Free*. Julia Gibney.

17. Australian Institute of Health and Welfare. (n.d.). *Health of young people*. Available at: https://www.aihw.gov.au/reports/children-youth/health-of-young-people.

18. Australian Bureau of Statistics. (2023). *National study of mental health and wellbeing: Latest release 2020-2022*. Available at: https://www.abs.gov.au/statistics/health/mental-health/national-study-mental-health-and-wellbeing/latest-release.

19. Australian Bureau of Statistics. (2023). *National study of mental health and wellbeing: Latest release 2020-2022*. Available at: https://www.abs.gov.au/statistics/health/mental-health/national-study-mental-health-and-wellbeing/2020-2022.

20. Duckworth, A. (2017). *GRIT: Why Passion and Resilience are the Secrets to Success*. London: Vermilion.

21. Haidt, J. (2024). *The Anxious Generation: How the great rewiring of childhood is causing an epidemic of mental illness*. Penguin.

22. Goldin, C. D. (2021). *Career and Family : women's century-long journey toward equity*. Princeton, New Jersey: Princeton University Press.

References

23. Dweck, C. (2006). *Mindset: The new psychology of success.* New York: Random House.

24. Virtue, D. (n.d.). *Boundaries are part of self-care. They are healthy, normal, and necessary.* Available at: https://www.azquotes.com/quote/810351.

25. Heeks, R. (2021). *From Digital Divide to Digital Justice in the Global South: Conceptualising Adverse Digital Incorporation.* [online] arXiv.org. doi:https://doi.org/10.48550/arXiv.2108.09783.

26. Sarkar, A.R. (2024). *Outrage after Australian news channel uses doctored image of woman MP.* [online] The Independent. Available at: https://www.independent.co.uk/news/world/australasia/georgie-purcell-nine-news-doctored-image-b2487044.html [Accessed 01 March 2024].

27. Bradley, A. (2023). *The hatred and vitriol Jacinda Ardern endured 'would affect anybody'.* RNZ Politics. Available at: https://www.rnz.co.nz/news/political/482761/the-hatred-and-vitriol-jacinda-ardern-endured-would-affect-anybody.

28. Measuring perceptions of equality for men and women in leadership. (2020). Available at: https://www.womenpoliticalleaders.org/wp-content/uploads/2020/11/The-Reykjavik-Index-for-Leadership-2020-Report-2-1.pdf.

29. Petrecca, L. (2023). *AARP Survey: More than 70% of women 50+ feel pressure to live up to beauty standards dictated by media.* Available at: https://www.aarp.org/entertainment/style-trends/info-2023/women-beauty-standards.html.

30. Handford, M., and Gee, J.P. (Eds.). (2023). *The Routledge Handbook of Discourse Analysis* (2nd ed.). Routledge. https://doi.org/10.4324/9781003035244.

31. Mills, S. (2003). *Gender and Politeness.* Cambridge: Cambridge University Press.

32. Holmes, J. (1995). *Women, Men and Politeness* (1st ed.). London: Routledge.

33. Tannen, D. (1994). *Gender and Discourse.* Oxford: Oxford University Press.

34. Tannen, D. (2001). *Talking from 9 to 5: Women and Men at Work.* HarperCollins.

35. Capanna-Hodge, D.R. (2024). *Neurotypical vs Neurodivergent Communication: Embracing Diversity in Dialogue.* [online] Dr. Roseann. Available at: https://drroseann.com/neurotypical-vs-neurodivergent-communication-embracing-diversity-in-dialogue/.

36. Blundell, A. (2023). *The Gender Penalty: Turning obstacles into opportunities for women at work.* BACCA House Press.

37. Kay, C. (2024). *Gender Differences in Communication | CK and CO.* [online] CK and CO. Available at: https://thinkck.com/gender-differences-in-communication/.

38. Brown, B. (2010). *The Gifts of Imperfection: Let Go of Who You Think You're Supposed to Be and Embrace Who You Are.* Center City, Minn.: Hazelden.

39. Gibney, J. (2023). *Break Free.* Julia Gibney.

40. Tawwab, N. G. (2021). *Set Boundaries, Find Peace: A Guide to Reclaiming Yourself.* Penguin Publishing Group.

41. Ely, R. J., Ibarra, H., and Kolb, D. M. (2011). *Taking gender into account: Theory and design for women's leadership development programs.* Academy of Management Learning & Education, 10(3), 474-493.

42. Hall, Lydia (nd). *25 Quotes About Setting Boundaries in Your Life.* Available at: https://minimalistathome.com/quotes-about-setting-boundaries/.

43. The Guardian. (2025, March 6). Australian men still do 50% less housework than women, new data shows. Available at: https://www.theguardian.com/world/2025/mar/06/australian-men-housework-statistics-domestic-labour-hilda-data.

44. Wilkins, R, Botha, F, Lass, I & Peyton, K. (2025). *HILDA survey shows inequality rises to a high*, University of Melbourne. Available at: https://www.unimelb.edu.au/newsroom/news/2025/march/hilda-shows-inequality-rises-to-a-high.

45. Ferrara, A. P., & Vergara, D. P. (2024). *Theorizing mankeeping: The male friendship recession and women's associated labor as a structural component of gender inequality.* Psychology of Men & Masculinities, 25(4), 391–401. https://doi.org/10.1037/men0000494.

References

46. Workplace Gender Equality Agency (WGEA). (2024). *Gender pay gap data*. Available at: https://www.wgea.gov.au/pay-and-gender/gender-pay-gap-data.

47. Mozahem, N.A, Masri, M.E.N, Najm, N.M and Saleh, S.S. (2021). How Gender Differences in Entitlement and Apprehension Manifest Themselves in Negotiation | Group Decision and Negotiation. Springer.com. Group Decision and Negotiation 30:587-610 https://doi.org/10/1007/s10726-021-09724-3.

48. Tannen, D. (1990). *You Just Don't Understand: Women and men in conversation*. New York: William Morrow.

49. Australian Government - Fair Work Ombudsman (2025). *Bullying, sexual harassment and discrimination at work*. Available at: https://www.fairwork.gov.au/employment-conditions/bullying-sexual-harassment-and-discrimination-at-work/bullying-in-the-workplace.

50. Federal Register of Legislation. (2025). *Fair Work Act (Cth) 2009*. Available at: https://www.legislation.gov.au/C2009A00028/latest/versions.

51. Federal Register of Legislation. (2024). *Sex Discrimination Act (Cth) 1984 Section 28A*. Available at: https://www.legislation.gov.au/C2004A02868/latest/text.

52. Carnegie, D. (1998). *How to win friends and influence people,* Pocket Books.

53. Sander, L. (2011). *The limbic system and its historical evolution.* Accessed through ResearchGate. Available at: https://www.researchgate.net/publication/51920788_The_Limbic_System_Conception_and_Its_Historical_Evolution/figures?lo=1.

54. Peters, S. (2012). *The Chimp Paradox: The mind management program to help you achieve success, confidence, and happiness*. London: Vermilion, An Imprint of Ebury Publishing.

55. Siegel, D.J. (1999). *The Developing Mind: How relationships and the brain interact to shape who we are*. S.L.: Guilford.

56. Mackay, H. (2014). *The Art of Belonging*. Sydney, N.S.W.: Pan Macmillan.

57. Hall, L. (n.d.). 25 *Quotes About Setting Boundaries in Your Life*. Available at: https://minimalistathome.com/quotes-about-setting-boundaries/.

58. Ray, R. (2021). *Setting Boundaries*. Macmillan Australia.
59. Ernst, F. (1971). *OK Matrix*. Available at: https://ernstokcorral.com/.
60. Karpman, S.B. (1968). *Fairy Tales and Script Drama Analysis*. Transactional Analysis Bulletin, Vol 7, No 26, April 1968.
61. Emerald, D. (2016). *The Power of TED* (The Empowerment Dynamic)*. Bainbridge Island, Wa: Polaris Publishing.
62. Angelou, M. (2011). *The Complete Collected Poems of Maya Angelou*. Random House.
63. Melfi, T. (2016). *Hidden Figures*. USA: Twentieth Century Fox.
64. Taflaga, M. (2015, March 4). *Who knew that toilets would have such a complicated history?* Museum of Australian Democracy. Available at: https://www.moadoph.gov.au/explore/stories/heritage/who-knew-that-toilets-would-have-such-a-complicated-history.
65. Khalil, D. (2021). *Women in STEM: Exploring the Stereotypes*. [online] USM Digital Commons. Available at: https://digitalcommons.usm.maine.edu/etd/411/ [Accessed 6 Feb. 2025].
66. Blundell, A. (2023). *The Gender Penalty*. BACCA House Press.
67. McKinsey & Company. (2020). *Diversity wins: How inclusion matters*. McKinsey & Company. Available at: https://www.mckinsey.com/featured-insights/diversity-and-inclusion/diversity-wins-how-inclusion-matters.
68. First Round Capital. (2015). *First Round 10 Year Project*. [online] First Round 10 Year Project. Available at: https://10years.firstround.com.
69. Lonergan, P. (2020). *Women face 'double-bind' when applying for jobs in male-dominated fields*. University of Toronto. Available at: https://www.utoronto.ca/news/women-face-double-bind-when-applying-jobs-male-dominated-fields-u-t-researchers-find.
70. Hall, W. and Schmader, T. (2019). *When Women Thrive in Male-dominated Workplaces*. Society for Personality and Social Psychology (SPSP). Available at: https://spsp.org/news-center/character-context-blog/ at: https://sciencegenderequity.org.au/ when-women-thrive-male-dominated-workplaces.

References

71. He, J.C. and Kang, S.K. (2020). Covering in Cover Letters: Gender and Self-Presentation in Job Applications. *Academy of Management Journal*, 64(4). doi:https://doi.org/10.5465/amj.2018.1280.

72. Greska, L. (2023). Women in academia: Why and where does the pipeline leak, and how can we fix it? 4, pp.102–109. doi:https://doi.org/10.38105/spr.xmvdiojee1.

73. Blundell, A. (2023). *The Gender Penalty*, BACCA House Press.

74. Tandrayen-Ragoobur, V. and Gokulsing, D. (2021). Gender gap in STEM education and career choices: what matters? *Journal of Applied Research in Higher Education*, 14(3), pp.1021–1040. doi:https://doi.org/10.1108/jarhe-09-2019-0235.

75. Baron-Cohen, S. (2021). *The Pattern Seekers: A New Theory of Human Invention*. Allen Lane.

76. Newsom, J. S., Scully, R. K., Booker, C., Davis, G., and Couric, K. (2012). *Miss Representation*. [Documentary]. New York, NY: Virgil Films.

77. World Economic Forum. (2023). *Gender gaps in the workforce - Global Gender Gap Report 2023*. [online] World Economic Forum. Available at: https://www.weforum.org/reports/global-gender-gap-report-2023.

78. Workplace Gender Equality Agency. (2024*). WGEA Data Explorer | WGEA*. [online] www.wgea.gov.au. Available at: https://www.wgea.gov.au/data-statistics/data-explorer.

79. SAGE. (n.d.). *Science in Australia Gender Equity*. [online] Available at: https://sciencegenderequity.org.au/.

80. Diversity Council Australia. (n.d.) *Home - Diversity Council Australia*. Available at: https://www.dca.org.au.

81. Zalis, S. (2019). Power Of The Pack: Women Who Support Women Are More Successful. *Forbes*. [online] 7 Mar. Available at: https://www.forbes.com/sites/shelleyzalis/2019/03/06/power-of-the-pack-women-who-support-women-are-more-successful/.

82. Workplace Gender Equality Agency (WGEA). (2024). *WGEA Gender Equality Scorecard 2023-2024*. Retrieved from https://www.wgea.gov.au/publications/australias-gender-equality-scorecard.

83. Morgan, B. (2022). *Solving the Part-Time Puzzle: How to decrease your hours, increase your impact and thrive in your part-time role.* Inva Pty Ltd.

84. Fisher, J. (n.d.) *Improve Your Conversations.* Available at: https://www.jeffersonfisher.com.

85. Bailey, L. H. (1935). *The Gardener's Companion.* Macmillan.

86. Department of the Prime Minister and Cabinet. (2023). *Foundation: Gender attitudes and stereotypes | Working for Women.* Australian Government. Available at: https://www.genderequality.gov.au/foundation-gender-attitudes-and-stereotypes.

87. Deloitte Access Economics. (2022). *Breaking The Norm: Unleashing Australia's economic potential.* Deloitte. Available at: https://www.deloitte.com/au/en/services/financial-advisory/blogs/breaking-the-norm-unleashing-australias-economic-potential.html.

88. Exley, C. L., & Kessler, J. B. (2021). *The gender gap in self-promotion* (Working Paper No. 26345). National Bureau of Economic Research. Available at: https://www.nber.org/system/files/working_papers/w26345/w26345.pdf.

89. Study Finds. (2023, April 7). *What is imposter syndrome? Women more likely to feel like 'phonies' than men.* Available at: https://studyfinds.org/what-is-imposter-syndrome/.

90. Hall, C. (2021). *Women Are Facing Greater Interruption Challenges with Remote Work Than Their Male Colleagues.* [online] UConn Today. Available at: https://today.uconn.edu/2021/12/women-are-facing-greater-interruption-challenges-with-remote-work-than-their-male-colleagues/.

91. Boavida, B. (2024). *The science is in: Interruptions Kill Productivity and Increase Stress (with sources).* [online] Workjoy.co. Available at: https://workjoy.co/blog/scientific-research-notifications-and-interruptions-negatively-affect-work#interruptions-of-44-seconds-triple-the-rate-of-errors-and-small-interruptions-can-lead-to-double-or-triple-the-rates-of-errors-on-the-main-task.

92. Edelman (2024). *Edelman Trust Barometer.* [online] Edelman. Available at: https://www.edelman.com/trust/trust-barometer.

References

93. TeamStage. (2024). Leadership statistics: Leadership Statistics: Demographics and Development in 2024. Available at: https://teamstage.io/leadership-statistics/.

94. Nguyen, J. (2024). *82 per cent of CEO pipeline roles are currently held by men, research finds*. Retrieved from https://www.hrmonline.com.au/culture-leadership/82-per-cent-of-ceo-pipeline-roles-held-by-men/.

95. Workplace Gender Equality Agency (WGEA). (2019). *International Women's Day 2019: Key facts about women and work*. Retrieved from https://www.wgea.gov.au/newsroom/international-womens-day-2019-key-facts-about-women-and-work.

96. Haycock, L. (2022). *The cost to hire an employee might be higher than you think*. [online] HRM online. Available at: https://www.hrmonline.com.au/section/featured/cost-of-hiring-new-employee/.

97. Bryant-Norved, M. (2022). *Understanding true costs of rising staff turn over*. [online] Available at: https://www.hcamag.com/au/specialisation/employee-engagement/understanding-true-costs-of-rising-staff-turnover/411095.

98. MacKenzie, K. (2019). *The cost of replacing an employee — it's more than you think | Workable*. [online] Recruiting Resources: How to Recruit and Hire Better. Available at: https://resources.workable.com/stories-and-insights/the-cost-of-replacing-an-employee.

99. Westfall, B. (2017). 5 Benefits (Yes, Benefits) of High Employee Turnover. [online] Software Advice. Available at: https://www.softwareadvice.com/resources/employee-turnover-benefits/.

100. Wholley, M. (2023). *7 Surprising Benefits of Employee Turnover | ClearCompany*. [online] blog.clearcompany.com. Available at: https://blog.clearcompany.com/benefits-of-employee-turnover.

101. Baron-Cohen, S. (2012). *The Science of Evil: On Empathy and the Origins of Cruelty*. Basic Books.

102. Goleman, D. (1995). *Emotional Intelligence: Why It Can Matter More Than IQ*. NY, New York: Bantam Books.

103. Zakolyukina, A., Tayan, B., O'Reilly, C. and Larcker, D. (2021). Are Narcissistic CEOs All That Bad? [online] The Harvard Law School Forum on Corporate Governance. Available at: https://corpgov.law.harvard.edu/2021/10/25/are-narcissistic-ceos-all-that-bad/.

104. Australian Government. (2024). *2024 Status of Women Report Card*. [online] Pmc.gov.au. Available at: https://ministers.pmc.gov.au/gallagher/2024/national-strategy-for-gender-equality.

105. Field, E., Krivkovich, A., Kügele, S., Robinson, N. and Yee, L. (2023). *Women in the Workplace 2023*. [online] McKinsey & Company. Available at: https://www.mckinsey.com/capabilities/people-and-organizational-performance/our-insights/women-in-the-workplace-2023.

106. Apple Podcasts. (2025). *The Jefferson Fisher Podcast*. [online] Available at: https://podcasts.apple.com/us/podcast/the-jefferson-fisher-podcast/id1754592060 [Accessed 6 Feb. 2025].

107. Winters, M. (2020). *Inclusive Conversations: fostering equity, empathy, and belonging across differences*. Oakland, Ca: Berrett-Koehler Publishers.

108. Apple Podcasts. (2023). *TriviumU: Timeless Training for Professional Communicators*. [online] Available at: https://podcasts.apple.com/us/podcast/triviumu-timeless-training-for-professional-communicators/id1689266470 [Accessed 6 Feb. 2025].

109. Australian Government. (2011). *Federal Register of Legislation — Work Health Safety Act 2011*. [online] Available at https://www.legislation.gov.au/C2011A00137/latest/text

110. Neff, K.D. and Dahm, K.A. (2015). Self-Compassion: What It Is, What It Does, and How It Relates to Mindfulness. *Handbook of Mindfulness and Self-Regulation*, pp.121–137. doi:https://doi.org/10.1007/978-1-4939-2263-5_10.

111. Norville, D. (2007). *Thank You Power: Making the science of gratitude work for you*. Nashville, Tennessee: Thomas Nelson.

112. Tilo, D. (2022*). 75% of Australians aren't using their annual leave*. [online] www.hcamag.com. Available at: https://www.hcamag.com/au/specialisation/benefits/75-of-australians-arent-using-their-annual-leave/424720.

113. Stanier, M. B. (2022). *How to begin: Start doing something that matters*. Vancouver, British Columbia: Page Two.

114. Erikson, T. (2019). *Surrounded by Idiots*. [S.I.]: St. Martin's Publishing Group.

References

115. Quotes and sayings. (2022). *The Best 20 Daniel Goleman Quotes - quotes and sayings - Medium.* [online] Medium. Available at: https://quotesandsayings.medium.com/the-best-20-daniel-goleman-quotes-85cede8bcf29.

116. Haidt, J. (2024). *The Anxious Generation: How the great rewiring of childhood is causing an epidemic of mental illness.* Penguin.

117. Winfrey, O. (2014). *What I know for sure.* Flatiron Books.

118. Zack, D. (2010). *Networking for people who hate networking: A field guide for introverts, the overwhelmed, and the underconnected.* Berrett-Koehler Publishers.

119. Clark, D. (2022). *The Long Game: How to be a long-term thinker in a short-term world.* Boston, Ma: Harvard Business Review Press.

120. Varol, O. (2023). *Awaken Your Genius: Escape conformity, ignite creativity, and become extraordinary.* PublicAffairs.

121. Zander, R. S. and Zander, B. (2000). *The Art of Possibility: Transforming professional and personal life.* Harvard Business School Press.

www.ingramcontent.com/pod-product-compliance
Lightning Source LLC
Chambersburg PA
CBHW071954290426
44109CB00018B/2022